"Hits all of us right where we live."

"*Living With Your Conscience Without Going Crazy* is for the many men and women whose conscience is cluttered with guilt over things they may or may not be responsible for. Joel's humorous approach makes easy reading as he leads you on a journey to resolve the guilt resulting in the freedom of a clear conscience."

Florence Littauer
Speaker and Bestselling Author

"With wit and disarming style, Joel Freeman explains the many benefits that come from a clear conscience. He offers refreshing insights on a subject that hits all of us right where we live."

Dr. D. James Kennedy
President, Evangelism Explosion

"'Conscience is that still, small voice that tells us that someone is looking.' Alas, this is true. In the sensitive soul, the voice of conscience is the voice of God. But of course, we must not lose this blessed and frightening gift, a sensitive conscience. Joel Freeman, in this perceptive work, tells us how to live with—yes, how to retain, even develop—spiritual sensitivity. His book is 'must reading' for all in this insouciant day."

Dr. David Breese
President, Christian Destiny, Inc.

"From his unique style and perspective, Joel Freeman exposes the human conscience. He asks readers to look at their own conscience with both laughter and conviction. The conscience has an intricate function in God's design of human beings. Making peace with our conscience God's way is necessary for healthy Christian living. Freeman's book is a source of reflection and insight on this important topic."

Paul Meier, M.D.
Minirth-Meier Clinic

"Vast numbers of people struggle every day under the weight of guilt and bondage. Freedom from a guilty conscience is ultimately found when we learn how to let Christ live in and through us. Using humor, personal vulnerability and tough-minded insights, Joel Freeman does a great job of showing how a life in grace relates to freedom in your conscience. I heartily recommend this book to anyone who is wrestling with his or her conscience."

Malcolm Smith
Bible Teacher

"Integrity, ethics, conscience. These attributes are sorely lacking, not only in the world today, but within the church as well! Joel's book gently confronts the *real* issues which the church faces today. Rationalization and excuses have replaced truth and repentance which Joel so poignantly entitles 'weasel clauses.' *Living With Your Conscience* is easy to read but hard to digest...I recommend it heartily for all who desire to remove the 'sludge' from their Christian walk.

George Otis
President, High Adventure Ministries

"Joel makes it easy with his wit, humor and down to earth philosophy to do it God's way. Keeping short accounts with God and people helps us to keep biblical perspectives in mind. When God forgives, He forgets, and we also should do the same, moving on to the goal of living a godly life, moment by moment. It's so simple to do it God's way, sometimes it's just not so easy."

Margaret Jensen
Speaker and Bestselling Author

"It was a pleasure to review and read your new book. Reading your book brought back many wonderful memories. I have prayed with many people during my years of ministry and I always encouraged them to always keep their eyes on the 'goal'; and never to look in the rear view mirror 'lest they go in the ditch.' Congratulations on this fine book and my prayer is that it will bless many people in the years that lie ahead."

Rex Humbard
Cathedral of Tomorrow

Living With Your Conscience

WITHOUT GOING CRAZY

JOEL A. FREEMAN

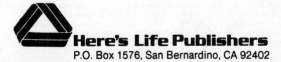

Here's Life Publishers
P.O. Box 1576, San Bernardino, CA 92402

First printing, July 1989

Published by
HERE'S LIFE PUBLISHERS, INC.
P. O. Box 1576
San Bernardino, CA 92402

Library of Congress Cataloging-in-Publication Data
Freeman, Joel A., 1954-
　　Living with your conscience without going crazy / Joel A. Freeman.
　　　　p.　　　cm.
　　ISBN 0-89840-251-4
　　1. Conscience — Religious aspects — Christianity.　　2. Christian
life — 1960- .　I. Title.
BJ1278.C66F74　　1989
241'.1 — dc 19　　　　　　　　　　　89-30708
　　　　　　　　　　　　　　　　　　　　　CIP

Unless otherwise indicated, Scripture quotations are from the *King James Version.*

Scripture quotations designated NIV are from *The Holy Bible: New International Version,* © 1973, 1978, 1984 by the International Bible Society. Published by Zondervan Bible Publishers, Grand Rapids, Michigan.

Scripture quotations designated TEV are from *The Good News Bible: Today's English Version,* © 1966, 1971, 1976 by the American Bible Society. Published by Thomas Nelson Publishers, Nashville, Tennessee.

Unless specifically identified as factual, all names have been fictionalized for protection and privacy.

For More Information, Write:
L.I.F.E. — P.O. Box A399, Sydney South 2000, Australia
Campus Crusade for Christ of Canada — Box 300, Vancouver, B.C., V6C 2X3, Canada
Campus Crusade for Christ — Pearl Assurance House, 4 Temple Row, Birmingham, B2 5HG, England
Lay Institute for Evangelism — P.O. Box 8786, Auckland 3, New Zealand
Campus Crusade for Christ — P.O. Box 240, Colombo Court Post Office, Singapore 9117
Great Commission Movement of Nigeria — P.O. Box 500, Jos, Plateau State Nigeria, West Africa
Campus Crusade for Christ International — Arrowhead Springs, San Bernardino, CA 92414, U.S.A.

To my precious parents,
Arthur and Katherine Freeman

Acknowledgments

To God. If it wasn't for His mercies, I'd be consumed.

Special thanks to my wonderful wife, Laurie, and my sons, David and Jesse. Your support and understanding have been immeasurable. I appreciate the behind-the-scenes humor, hard work and willingness to love. I have been blessed with a great family.

Thanks to each and every member of Stillmeadow Christian Church for graciously allowing me to take time away from you to write and travel. Most pastors would give anything to have an unselfish congregation like you! You are a wild and crazy bunch!

Thanks to Melanie Dixon, my secretary. Your uncanny ability to translate my "chicken scratchings" into legible copy is absolutely amazing.

Thanks to Dan Benson, my editorial director, and Barbara Sherrill, the project editor. You both have been blessed with the ability to take an imperfect manuscript and increase its life-changing quality.

Thanks to all who helped proofread the original draft of this book: Stephen, Angie, George, Dad, Mom and Bernice. Dawn was an exceptional help.

And finally, thanks to Bert and Ferd. I plan to keep you guys busy!

Contents

Foreword

Albert Einstein said that real human progress depended on conscience. That includes individual progress as well as progress in society. It includes you and me and what we do with our lives.

Conscience can mean progress . . . in building character . . . in achieving goals . . . in relating to other people . . . in handling the defeats and disasters of life . . . in making a life as well as a living.

George Washington called conscience "that little spark of celestial fire." Put the fire out and you lose warmth and light and direction and hope.

This book is about progress and hope.

It's about you and your conscience.

Take it seriously. The future you save will be your own.

Warren W. Wiersbe
General Director
Good News Broadcasting Association

Horror Stories

Has the gift of blab ever gotten you into trouble?

Deep trouble?

Has your mental gymnastics exercise program ever included "jumping to conclusions" and "throwing temper tantrums"?

Do you hate being in the presence of phonies?

Have you ever focused your hatred upon a number-one jerk?

Have you ever tried to build your success upon someone else's defeat?

Have you ever struggled with the highs and lows of guilt addiction?

Does your conscience have an 8th degree black belt?

   If you answered *yes* to any of these questions, this book is for you. Hey, join the club. I know a bunch of people who can join me in answering *yes* to every one of those questions. Even though I have an all-consuming desire to serve God in an honorable, fervent manner, sometimes I, like many others, feel like a hypocrite and a fraud — professing one thing while experiencing another.

   As a radio talk show host, pastor and trained counselor, I have counseled literally hundreds of people over the years. Many have expressed acute agony over the guilt ex-

11

perienced because of the frightening disparity between their actual emotional state and their perception of the way they ought to be. It's like living in "no-man's-land."

It's plain and simple. Sometimes we lack *integrity*. Sometimes we feel like we're going crazy. We're not proud of it—but that's reality.

I'm not, however, content with staying in a rut. How about you? I want to grow—God's way. There's a poster hanging above my younger son's bed that says it all: *God loves me just the way I am and too much to let me stay that way.* How true! That's what it's all about.

Warning. *This is a serious book.* Everyone has *heard* a "horror story." You know the kind—the respected minister suddenly leaves his wife and kids, quits the ministry and moves in with another woman. Everyone is shocked. It was discovered that the affair had been in the works for over a year, complete with secret meetings and clandestine rendezvous at various motels. And he seemed to be so sincere. Lipsmacking, finger-wagging, head-shaking scandal.

What about the "Christian" businessman who has all the appearances of a genteel rip-off artist? He tools down the highway in his vehicle, complete with "Honk if You Love Jesus" and "Christians Aren't Perfect, Just Forgiven" bumper stickers. Anyone who deals with him on any level deeper than his saccharine smile and bionic handshake is left with a sour taste and feels used. He leaves a trail of people who stock their bookshelves with volumes on the subject of forgiveness.

Or how about the girl who was a typical (whatever that means) teenager? You watched her grow up and remember her as a vivacious, fun-loving youngster, but something happened. Almost overnight, it seemed, she turned into a sullen, obstinate person. The transformation was frightening. Right around fifteen years of age, you figure. One morning you wake up to see the bold print head-lines screaming, *Local Girl Dies in Suicide Pact.* You become unnerved. Shattered. What went wrong? Why? Why? Her internal world must've been a confused mess.

This is a challenging book. Everyone has *lived* a "horror story." You know what I mean—the kind where you lie on the floor, drawn up in fetal position, sobbing until there are no tears left. A cruel verbal attack from someone you thought was a dear friend? Divorce? Rebellious son or daughter? Fired from your job? Jilted by a girlfriend or boyfriend? You fill in the blanks.

This is a probing book. Everyone has *told* a "horror story." It's no laughing matter. Ignoring tons of scriptural mandates about the dangers of judging and the wily, un-tameable nature of the tongue, you listened to some juicy gossip about another person. It felt so good to hear that someone else had "blown it." You had thought all along that underneath the exterior goody-two-shoes image of that in-dividual was a two-faced hypocrite. And now what you've heard about him has justified your suspicions. The spot-light was shifted from you and your own imperfections to someone else. You couldn't wait to blab it to some acquain-tance, adding a few embellishments of your own.

Many of us have settled on the *big* issues. Embez-zlement. Murder. Sexual immorality. Drugs. Legalism or the fear of getting-caught-with-your-pants-down may keep us from blatant sins.

But what about the "tiny" things? What can a series of small compromises do to the course of our lives? Are there tangible, positive benefits that flow from a life of in-tegrity—one characterized by a clear conscience?

A life of integrity. Is it dull? Is it a boring, rule-laden endeavor? Is it an unattainable goal? Is it one step forward, thirteen steps backwards? Just how *do* you live with your conscience without going crazy?

I've done a lot of contemplating on those issues, the bulk of which you now hold in your hands. But before addressing those questions and more, I want to thank God for the many people who have contributed to my life and my way of thinking. In the 13th century, Bernard of Clairvaux said, "We are like dwarves on the shoulders of giants . . . "

My writings have been influenced by such "giants" of the past as Andrew Murray, Oswald Chambers, Watchman Nee, C. S. Lewis, A. W. Tozer, and a host of others. Many of my contemporaries, some of whom are mentioned in this book, have also supplied their "shoulders" for me to "stand upon."

Bert and Ferd know them all.

Joel A. Freeman, M.S.
P. O. Box 2757
Columbia, Maryland 21045

ONE

Another Day
Shot to Heaven

*It is curious—curious that physical courage
should be so common in the world
and moral courage so rare.*
—Mark Twain

She was young, probably in her early twenties. Her straight, dark hair hung down to a red, semi-revealing halter top and framed a rather fine-featured, pretty face that was lined with boredom. Her smile seemed forced, but inviting. But what about those cold, calculating, lifeless eyes? Steel-blue. Penetrating. She seemed to be looking through him—beyond him.

There he was, all alone, with his car idling pleasantly while stopped at a red light, minding his own business. Michael, a hard-working, God-fearing, father-of-four, mow-the-lawn-every-Saturday insurance broker, was at an all-American intersection. You know, the kind with a McDonalds to the right, a hardware store on the left and a fire station straight ahead.

All of a sudden, out of nowhere she came. It must've been from his blind spot. He didn't see her until a tapping

15

noise on the passenger side window caused him to turn suddenly and look. She made a circular movement with her
hand indicating that she wanted him to roll the window
down. Involuntarily, he reached over and cranked the
lever — awkwardly straining to comply.

The first question out of her mouth stunned him.
(For the sake of decency we will not print what she said.)
He had always considered himself to be a fairly unshock-
able person, but he was shocked. It was as if someone had
sucker-punched him in the solar plexus.

His mind jerked instantly into high gear with a
hundred rationalizations bombarding him from all sides.
*Here's your opportunity. No one will ever find out. She is
rather cute. C'mon, you can receive God's forgiveness afterwards. Loosen up, dummy. You've walked the "straight and
narrow" for a long time now. How about a slight,
pleasurable detour?*

For what seemed like an eternity, Michael stared
back at her. Their eye contact probably lasted no more than
one whole second. "No, thank you," he responded, trying
hard to conjure up a tone of voice that sounded non-
judgmental, yet firm.

Without changing her facial expression, she turned
and walked to the rear of the car. Whew, that was too close
for comfort! His emotions turned to Jell-O. He felt like the
moments following a near head-on collision with another
vehicle: dazed; relieved; panicky; acutely aware of his mortality.

He reached shakily up to his rear-view mirror, ad-
justing it so he could see where she was going. The guy
behind him in the blue sedan was watching her too. After
a brief verbal exchange at the other guy's passenger window, she hopped in. The light turned green.

Michael turned left on the double-laned boulevard.

The guy in the blue sedan wasted no time as he sped around and then ahead of him. Michael caught a glimpse of her gazing vacantly out of the window. He tried as best he could to follow them, but soon lost sight of the car. His mind continued to race.

Are they going to a motel that rents by the hour? To her apartment? To a secluded park? Hey, wait a minute! Why am I so curious? Am I getting some kind of vicarious thrill out of this whole thing?

Did Michael handle this situation with integrity? Oh, sure, he said *no* to temptation, but why did he feel a twinge of regret for saying no? Why did he even have second thoughts? Where did the adrenalin come from?

Integrity. Tough stuff. Another day shot to heaven.

It was a "typical" day at the office. Phone calls to be returned. Reports to be drafted. A general atmosphere of tension.

Saundra, a pleasant, professionally attired woman in her thirties, was suddenly interrupted by the half-whisper of her respected co-worker, Harold.

"I need to talk to you real bad," he confided in hushed tones. "Can we get together at lunch time? I can't stand it any longer. I've got to talk to somebody real soon or I'm going to burst. You're the *only* person I can trust."

As Saundra went back to her task at hand, she smiled. *It sure feels good to be trusted.*

The morning passed quickly. Before she knew it, Harold was calling her name and they both settled down for a hearty lunch.

"It's Duane," Harold said. "I can't stand him."

Saundra knew Duane vaguely. He had been on the job for approximately a month. "What seems to be the problem?" she queried.

As Harold detailed the situation, Saundra listened intently with a genuine desire to help. Within a matter of minutes, however, she made the awkward conclusion that Harold was gossiping. It was the way he tore Duane down and built himself up. It was his tone of voice and demeaning spirit.

Several times Saundra attempted to interject thoughts that would objectify the situation, but to no avail. She soon realized that he wasn't really interested in a solution. She was merely a sounding board for his frustration. Harold kept plowing forward—full steam ahead!

She began to feel extremely uncomfortable. Harold wouldn't be talking like this if Duane were present. She didn't want to be unkind or represent an attitude of superiority, yet she didn't want to be a party to what was transpiring, either.

Should she keep quiet and not say a word in order to avoid injuring her working relationship with Harold? Or should she tell Harold to work out his differences with Duane—alone?

Perhaps she should gently stop him, admitting, "I have a real problem with listening to gossip. I love to hear every nasty, juicy bit of scandalous rumor. In fact, I have to slap my hand every time I stand in line at the grocery store checkout counter. While I'm waiting I have to fight the desire to read about Liz Taylor's latest UFO lover in one of those national sleaze journals. You see, I have a real tough time hearing negative things about other people when I'm not a part of the problem or a part of the solution. Thank you for understanding."

Integrity. Tough stuff. Another day shot to heaven.

Sharon, a woman in her mid-fifties, had been attending several months worth of meetings at the church I pastor. Her husband Jerry had come with her several times, but portrayed a general disinterest in spiritual matters. He was a no-nonsense, gruff, General Patton-type of guy. I was intrigued by him, and for some reason I had a desire to really get to know him.

One evening my wife Laurie and I were invited to their home for dinner. Laurie immediately joined Sharon in the kitchen. Jerry and I settled down in the living room. In short order we discovered a common interest—hunting. We discussed such esoteric subjects as muzzle velocity, bullet weights and shell reloading techniques. He showed me his gun cabinet. With near-reverential awe, I inspected each piece of his collection of firearms.

"By the way," he said as he watched me fondle his finely-etched double-barrelled shotgun, "how would you like to go rabbit hunting with me in a couple of weeks?"

"Hey, that would be great," I responded, thinking about the welcome break it would bring into my busy schedule.

"Good! I'll arrange a date with my friend who lives up near the Pennsylvania border. He owns a fruit orchard and there are plenty of good places to hunt on his land."

Then came the crucial question, "Do you have your hunting license?"

"Oh, sure," I said quickly. "No problem there. It'll be all taken care of."

Actually, I had no intention of getting my license. My rationalization gears were already whirring. *Hey, nobody's gonna check for my license. We'll be hunting on private land, anyway. Furthermore, why blow a twenty dollar bill for a lousy license that I probably won't have time to use for the rest of the season? What? Me worry? No problem!*

The rest of the evening went by quickly. All was well. Or so I thought.

I pulled into Jerry's driveway about 4 o'clock on the morning we were to go hunting. The early morning air was clear and crisp. His hound dogs knew what was on the agenda for the day. Their enthusiasm was catching.

After we exchanged some small talk, he asked, "Where's your hunting license?"

This took me by complete surprise. I didn't expect him to bring the subject up. Instinctively, I began to pat my pockets as if I was looking for my license. "Oh my gosh," I blurted, "I must've left it at home." Secretly I was hoping that he'd consider the forty extra minutes it would take to drive to my apartment a waste of time and say, "Oh, let's just forget about it."

But he didn't. Instead he made the dreaded statement, "OK, then, we'll drive to your house and pick it up."

Yikes! Why did he have to play this one by the book? My emotions bottomed out. *What's he gonna think of me when he finds out the truth? He'll probably lose all respect for me.* Suddenly I had a surge of hope. *Maybe I can find last year's license and put it in the plastic holder pinned to the back of my jacket. Sure, last year's license is a different color, but during the whole trip I'll position myself so that he'll never get a good look at my back. It'll be hard, but I can do it.*

I couldn't allow him to catch me in this lie. After all, he'd probably never come back to church and I'd be a laughing stock behind his closed doors. He'd say, "Sharon, are you going to hear that hypocritical, lying preacher again this Sunday? Don't waste your time. He's a phony!" I could almost hear those accusing words burning in my ears.

The pickup truck ride over to my apartment was one of the longest I've ever experienced. It was still dark, so he couldn't see the glum expression on my face. Upon our arrival, I walked purposefully up the steps and unlocked the door; once inside, however, nervous energy took over as I raced to the bedroom. I grabbed a flashlight, not wanting to wake my wife. Frantically I searched through my infamous junk drawer filled with maybe-it-will-come-in-handy-sometime treasures. Last year's license was not to be found.

I looked at the clock. Five minutes had elapsed. What was I to do? I buried my face in my hands. When everything else fails—tell the truth. The simple truth. Right? Wrong. At least not yet. I went to one more spot where it could be hidden. It wasn't there. Now it was time to really panic!

I walked back out to the truck. The light flickered on in the cab as I opened the door. I could see the expectant look in his eyes. Quickly I shut the door. I felt more comfortable in the darkness.

"Jerry," I said tentatively while looking straight ahead, "I lied to you. I do not have my hunting license. Please forgive me."

He started the truck and shifted into gear. Silence. I felt like a tiny grease spot. A little blob of quivering humanity.

We drove for a good ten minutes without talking. *What a stupid idiot! Why didn't I have the guts to tell him the truth right from the beginning? Why did I prolong the inevitable? I was forced to tell him the truth anyway. Why did I try to cover it up? I'm a poor excuse for a pastor. My credibility with him is shot to smithereens. Why doesn't he say something?*

He finally broke the silence. "We'll pick up a license at a sporting goods store that's on the way. Oh, by the way, don't let what just happened bother you. It's all going to work out." It was his way of accepting my apology.

I finally told him the truth, but did I do so only because I was caught? Why did I feel so guilty even after asking for and receiving forgiveness both from God and Jerry? Was I more concerned about Jerry's estimation of me than I was of God's? After all the Bible training, counseling and preaching experience I had, why did I succumb to the age-old trap of trying to cover up one lie with a bigger one?

Integrity. Tough stuff. Another day shot to heaven.

In the *Manufacturer's Handbook,* the Bible, the apostle Paul claimed that it is possible to do such incredible things as give our bodies to be burned, sell all we own and give the money to the poor, or have such faith that we could actually remove mountains—and still not possess divine love.

The same principle holds true with integrity. It is possible to return undeserved change given by the grocery store cashier, report every earned penny to the IRS, and drive at 54.9 mph in a 55 mph zone—and still not have genuine integrity.

"I'm depressed," I can hear someone groan. "I might as well stop reading now."

Don't give up. There's hope! I have discovered some wonderful principles that, when applied, can transform the lousiest attitude and can sharpen the blurriest focus. Instead of having our days shot to "hell" by the unexpected, unplanned-for circumstances, we can undergo an attitude change and can literally find ways to bleed the most impossible situations for every drop of spiritual maturity we can squeeze from it. Then we'll be ready to say, "Well, it's been another day shot to heaven. It's been filled with eternal value. Can't wait till tomorrow to learn more about integrity!"

Are you ready to grow together with me?

As we head into the next chapter, place your tongue firmly in your cheek, pull your Neurotics Anonymous membership card out of your wallet, look at it with a rather neurotic fondness and let's enter into a meeting that is about to be called to order. My card has already been presented.

Bert and Ferd will be there.

Points to Ponder

1. When was the last time you were confronted with a lack of integrity in your life? Try to remember what your innermost feelings were at that time.

2. Your past, present and future lapses from integrity are prime candidates for God's healing love and grace. As you read *Living With Your Conscience Without Going Crazy*, ask Him to help you apply the principles you will be learning.

TWO

Neurotics Anonymous

*I count him braver who overcomes his desires
than him who overcomes his enemies,
for the hardest victory is victory over self.*
—Aristotle

Picture this: An odd conglomeration of people attending a weekly Neurotics Anonymous (N.A.) meeting.

Peter wipes a few beads of perspiration from his forehead. Jacob, the moderator, nods his head in Peter's direction, affirming what Peter already knows. The moment of truth has arrived. It's his first time in attendance and now it's his turn.

He glances around at the informal circle of men and women and flashes one of those beatific PR smiles. Everyone responds warmly, even the austere ones like Elijah and Paul.

"Hello." His voice crackles and he clears his throat. He can feel himself blushing ever so slightly. "My name is Simon Peter and I'm a neurotic." There, he said it!

Peter feels like a duck on a pond—everything calm

above the water, but feet paddling furiously beneath the surface. *What am I doing here? Why is everybody looking at me? All right, enough already! Next. Let's get on with the program.*

"Welcome, Peter." The pleasant chorus of voices interrupts his disjointed train of thought. He nods in appreciation, looking quickly to King David on his left, hoping he'll catch the cue and take the dreadful spotlight away. It's David's turn.

As everyone is introducing himself, Peter looks around the dimly lit room. The air is stuffy. The basement wall is painted with your basic "vomit green" color. Most of the people are garden-variety-type neurotics.

Sure, the room is filled with ageless celebrities like the once complaining Jeremiah, the once angry Moses, the once bitter Naomi, the once cowardly Timothy, and the once workaholic Martha, but it still had taken a lot of guts for him to come. Hardly his idea of a scintillating evening. He had forced himself to attend as he had heard that this was a meeting filled with people faced with similar fears, insecurities and guilt feelings. Maybe someone will say something that will help. Who knows?

Suddenly all focus their attention on Jacob as he begins to speak. His voice is surprisingly gentle. "Welcome, everyone," he says while surveying the room. He sports a bushy head of white, curly hair with a shiny bald spot, front and center. He's quite a character. Wizened, olive brown skin. Hook nose. Deeply set, snappy eyes under the shadow of thick eyebrows. He gestures broadly as he talks.

"As many of you know, Abraham and Sarah were scheduled to talk this evening, but neither one could make it. So, I'll fill in for them.

"We're all here tonight because we recognize that we are neurotics. Left to ourselves, we struggle with unrealistic expectations, needless emotional stress and depression.

"Consequently, we don't make decisions or think thoughts that are based on integrity. I know. I've been there and I still struggle with it at times."

Most everyone murmurs in assent. Peter is captivated. His attention is riveted on Jacob.

"I distinctly remember when my twin brother Esau came to visit me. It was about nine or ten years after I had tricked him out of his birthright. Oh, do I remember that!" he exclaims while laughing heartily. "Esau wanted to slit my throat at the time. I barely escaped by the skin of my teeth.

"Well, anyway, nine or ten years later," he repeated, "I received the news that Esau wanted to visit me. Wow, was I ever scared! I began to panic. What was Esau thinking? Had the years increased his bitterness and hatred toward me? Was this a clever plot by Esau to gain my trust and then to torture me slowly?

"I didn't know what to do," he continued. "Immediately I began to pray. But, I wasn't too sure if God had heard me. Or, if He had heard me, why should He care? There was nothing about me that would warrant His protection. I was a low-down, nasty scumball.

"So, I devised a brilliant plan—just in case my prayers hadn't penetrated the roof of my tent. I separated my servants, sheep, goats and cattle into two equal groups. I figured that if Esau slaughtered me and confiscated my possessions I'd be giggling in my grave because he had only gotten half of all I owned. Brilliant? You'd better believe it!

"The next day Esau's caravan appeared over the top of a sand dune, and when he saw me, he leaped off his camel and ran to greet me. While he had me in a bear hug, I patted him down but couldn't find any weapons in his clothing.

All my fears were groundless."

Everyone in the room is transfixed and silent. The stillness of the room is punctuated by an occasional "Ooh" or "Ah" as all listen to Jacob graphically relate his extreme levels of neurosis during his championship wrestling match with an angel, his marriage to the wrong woman and other dramatic events.

Time flies. Before Peter knows it, the evening is almost gone and he is experiencing hope. If an unpredictable "wacko" like Jacob can make it, maybe he can too. What strikes Peter the most, though, is that God was so patient with Jacob although He knew in advance what a manipulator and liar he was. In fact, God actually gave Jacob a blessing before dealing with his wicked heart. Talk about integrity!

Join the Club

While I extricate my tongue from the inside of my cheek, I think about the many wild and crazy Bible characters who struggle with besetting sins and neurotic tendencies.

How about the psalms of David? At times David sounds like a blubbering idiot when he writes about persecution and his desire for vengeance. Or the moodiness of Jonah? His irrational fears caused him to soak in the gastric juices of a fish for three days. Or how about the unpredictability of Moses? Deep-seated rage motivated him to murder an Egyptian and strike the rock at an inopportune time.

The Bible pulls no punches when portraying its characters' dark, shadowy sides. But you know what? Each person had one thing in common—*an all-consuming passion to honor God.*

Neurotics Anonymous has a membership of more

modern individuals also. D. L. Moody, with his outbursts of anger behind closed doors, is a charter member. Charles Haddon Spurgeon, the prince of preachers, was immobilized periodically by severe depression and financial worries. Amy Carmichael, the faithful missionary to India, was stricken at times with discouragement. The list goes on with such notables as C. S. Lewis, Hudson Taylor and the 19th-century advocate of missions, Count Zinzendorf.

Legalistic tendencies. Temper flareups. Lust problems. Cowardice. Self-pity. Mood swings. Caustic attitudes. Hyper-spirituality. Self-deception. Dependent personality disorders. Martyr complexes. Yes, the people who have served God over the centuries have given place to many warped and distorted mental attitudes. Yet should this history of imperfection cause us to back off from the Lord and His mandates?

Perhaps we accept the invitation simply to play a role. The cheerful giver. The loving husband. The compassionate servant. The submissive wife. The humble giant. The second-miler. The uncompromising prophet. The busy worker. Whatever it is, we find our niche. Year after year we fulfill our duties. We're faithful, but there's no vim and vigor. There's no zest. There's no power, joy or grace. We feel worn out. Something's missing.

Consider instead a life of integrity. A life of true integrity doesn't mean that we have to become sourpuss-pickle-testers-in-a-pickle-factory. And it doesn't mean that we have to be a bunch of phony baloneys. *Au contraire!*

Instead, we live a life made up of moments. If we sin (God forbid), we confess it and move on to the next moment with a clear conscience, enthusiastically looking for opportunities to praise Him and encourage other pilgrims.

Moments of Integrity

Integrity is needed in all facets of society. Child-rearing. Behind the steering whell of a car. In our everyday conversations.

What about the church board? The person who tithes the most has the most clout. What about the secretary? It's difficult to answer the phone with a genuine, caring attitude for the 131st time this week. What about the salesperson? It's easy to fudge the details of the expense account, just a wee bit. Or what about the marital relationship? Pleasant and talkative in public, but surly and silent behind closed doors.

These situations and a host of others provide opportunities for us to be confronted by our obvious need for integrity. But what do we do after we discover our lack of integrity? Do we gaze within, entering into the paralysis of analysis, asking ourselves a ton of "Why" questions? Do we pump ourselves up with a bunch of self-help books and tape positive statements all over our bathroom mirrors? Do we neurotically beat ourselves up with self-pity and condemnation because of the naked truth about the disparity between the God-implanted desire for integrity and the dismal reality of our actual experiences?

What is integrity? And how can we live a life of integrity—the kind of life that doesn't contain hypocrisy or self-righteousness?

Bert and Ferd know.

Points to Ponder

1. Could you relate to any of the biblical characters at the Neurotics Anonymous meeting? Why or why not?

2. Do you see hope for your own situation in the contemplation of theirs, knowing about God's care for each of them?

THREE

UPtegrity – INtegrity – OUTegrity

Our confidence in Christ does not make us lazy, negligent or careless, but on the contrary it awakens us, urges us on, and makes us active in living righteous lives and doing good. There is no self-confidence to compare with this.
— Ulrich Zwingli

Uncompromising. Truthful. Whole. Complete. Honest. Sound. Loyal. Honorable. Virtuous. Moral. Any definition of *integrity* will include some of the aforementioned words. Wouldn't it be nice to be the perfect personification of those words—all the time?

Yes it would, but most of us are spectators in life. We obtain a vicarious thrill from those who go beyond the realm of normalcy. Life is like a game. The real excitement usually comes in participating, not watching. Oh, sure, there's safety in the spectator's seat. The arm chair quarterback experiences no cuts or bruises. It's easy to

decline the invitation to come down onto the playing field
when perched securely in the nosebleed section of the
grandstand. We can holler advice without having to personally or responsibly test the outcomes of our "bright
ideas."

Ask Job. He was experiencing all the luxury that life
had to offer. He owned 7,000 sheep, 3,000 camels, 500
teams of oxen, 500 donkeys, and he employed a vast number of servants. He was the richest person in the land of
Uz. No question about it, he led a charmed life. God blessed
everything he touched.

As the Bible tells it, God had a conversation with
Satan and pointed out that Job hated evil and was the
finest, purest man in all the earth. To which Satan scoffed,
"Yeah, why shouldn't he, when You've taken such good
care of him? You have always protected him and kept his
home and property from harm. You have prospered everything he does. He just sits around, watching life go by — look
how rich he is! No wonder he worships You! But if You were
to take away his wealth and harm his family, You'd see how
quickly he would curse You to Your face!"

God responded, in so many words, "I'm convinced
that Job is a man of integrity. He doesn't need warm, fuzzy
feelings to keep him happy. He has a firm understanding
of his pilgrim, just-passing-through status on earth. He
honors me with a positive, trustful attitude. I'll tell you
what, Satan, do anything you want to his property, his
family and his possessions — but don't lay a finger on Job."

Meanwhile, back at the ranch, Job is basking in the
sun's rays, oblivious to the fact that he is the center of such
controversy. Without his knowledge or permission, he has
just been enrolled in God's university. First class? Reality
101. He has been invited out of the audience and onto the
stage, out of the grandstand and onto the playing field.

The integrity of the individual is tested on the playing field. Having to work with an obnoxious person. Marriage—the one relationship that smokes out selfishness like none other. Outright persecution. A "wilderness experience"—no warm, fuzzy feelings for months. Tragedy—relative gets killed in a car accident. Prosperity—lulled into a state of false security and complacency. Criticism. The cyclic despair of sinful habits. Seductive temptation. Get the picture?

Do you want to retreat to the comfort of the grandstands? How about experiencing maturity through integrity? It will be worth the adjustments, the honesty and the pain.

The True Meaning of Integrity

The word *integrity* actually comes from the term *to integrate* which means to "bring together, incorporating parts into a whole."[1] *People of integrity, therefore, are those whose passion in life is for an unbroken, cooperative fellowship with the One who made them.* They are determined that nothing will break that communion. No stimulating temptation. No obnoxious person. No overwhelming distress. No unpleasant circumstance. No heady success.

People of integrity are consumed with the love for restoration and reconciliation. They weep when a marriage breaks up. They grieve when a church splits down the middle. They pray quietly when an enemy stumbles and falls. When two individuals are at odds, justifying their rights, those who are interested in "integration" take both parties by the hand in an encouraging manner, and in so many words say, "Come now, let us reason together. Let's work this out. Let's take our eyes off each other and focus upon Jesus."

I'm reminded of an article written by Henry G.

Bosch for the popular devotional booklet *Our Daily Bread*. His portrayal of deacon Brown aptly illustrates the lifestyle of one who loves true integrity. It is entitled "Good Gossip":

> Believe it or not, the word *gossip* once meant that a person was a "God-sib," or "a relative in the sight of God." The term was applied to "God-parents" who were expected to form a warm relationship with the family of a newborn child. In its early usage the term *gossip* thus came to mean "to confide something good."
>
> In an imaginary story, Smith and Jones attended the same church, but they never agreed on anything. In fact, they didn't even speak to each other. This worried deacon Brown, so he decided to intervene. He visited Smith and asked, "What do you think of Jones?" "He's the meanest crank around!" Smith replied. "But," said Brown, "you have to admit that he is very kind to his family." "Oh, sure, he's kind to his family."
>
> The next day deacon Brown went to Jones and said, "Smith said you were very kind to your family. What do you think of Smith?" "Oh, he's a scalawag!" "But you have to admit that he's very honest in business," replied Brown. "Yes, he is honest in business."
>
> Deacon Brown called on Smith again the next day. "Do you know that Jones says you are very honest in business?" "Well, of all things!" replied Smith. On Sunday, Smith and Jones nodded to each other in church, so Brown continued his "meddling." At the next annual business meeting of the church, Smith and Jones smiled, and finally they voted on the same side!
>
> We need more "gossips" like deacon Brown.[2]

The True Meaning of Dis-integrity

Before returning to Job, let's explore the flip side to the term *integrate*: the word *disintegrate*. Its definition includes the idea of breaking up or destroying the cohesion of a unit. It is used when referring to something whole or complete that is smashed, reducing it to fragmented particles. Kind of like taking a sledgehammer to a ceramic dish.

Any word, thought or deed that divides or scatters has its roots in *disintegration*. It's no wonder that Jesus said we are a part of a kingdom that either scatters or gathers with Him. There are no grey areas from His perspective.

Have you ever been the object of someone's intense hatred? Maybe a member in your church, a next door neighbor, a jealous co-worker or a relative who has for no apparent reason sought to destroy your reputation. Slowly but surely nasty rumors, innuendos and downright malicious gossip about your work habits or personal life begin to filter back to you.

You are bewildered. Where are the stories coming from? After careful investigation you discover the source. Anger wells up within. After calming down, you approach that person in a gentle manner, trying to discern the motivation behind each uncalled-for attack. To no avail. The individual cannot be dealt with on a rational level. He is extremely defensive and seems to be driven by a bizarre way of thinking that defies common sense or logic. The slanderous remarks continue. You gradually realize that you are dealing with one who lacks integrity — a person who is relating to an invisible system that scatters. He seems to be controlled by the need to destroy or expose the slightest flaw at any cost.

We Are What We Relate To

Thousands of years ago, Job had many chances to align himself with Satan and thereby *disintegrate* under the extreme pressures of his circumstances. But each time, he ultimately selected the option to be *integrated* into God's thoughts. He obviously had made the conscious choice to keep his heart tender toward Jehovah God long before his very existence was rocked by a series of unexpected disasters.

Even his wife, aghast at the tragedies, queried, "Are you still holding on to your integrity? Curse God and die!" (Job 2:9, NIV)

Without batting an eyelash, Job replied, "You are talking nonsense! When God sends us something good, we welcome it. How can we complain when He sends us trouble?" (Job 2:10, TEV)

In all his suffering, Job refused to allow Satan to separate him from the One to be trusted regardless of the circumstances. I don't want to trivialize the seriousness of the pain that Job's wife was experiencing, but she was obviously relating to a system of perception that was opposite to Job's.

Satan was here a long time before Job existed. The Bible mentions that he was kicked out of heaven like lightning and was declared to be the *kosmokrator*,[4] the ruler of this world. Along with one third of all the angels that left the celestial scene with him, Lucifer set up shop here in what is known as the *Kosmos*,[5] the world — which literally means "orderly arrangement."

Even though God is the sovereign ruler of the universe, Satan has been given certain jurisdiction. Our planet is the realm over which Satan acts and exerts his influence. He has initiated a system devoted to disintegration and yet paradoxically characterized by order. He and his demonic cohorts are united by one passion — to destroy Christ.

Some people have a hard time believing this. Let me introduce you to a small part of Satan's agenda and attitude:

● Open your eyes that you may see, O men of mildewed

minds, and listen to me ye bewildered millions!
- This is the age of Satan! Satan Rules the Earth!
- Cursed are the "lambs of God," for they shall be bled whiter than snow!
- He who turns the other cheek is a cowardly dog!
- There is no heaven of glory bright, and no hell where sinners roast . . . Here and now is our opportunity!
- Hate your enemies with a whole heart and if a man smite you on the cheek, SMASH him on the other! Smite him hip and thigh, for self-preservation is the highest law!
- Say to thine own heart, "I am my own redeemer."
- Why not really be honest and if you are going to create a god in your image, why not create that god as yourself?

The Satanic Bible[6]

If you open your eyes to it, the reality of kingdom warfare will hit you full in the face. Satan hates you if you're committed to the person and work of Jesus Christ. Don't ever forget that fact. He will pull every trick out of his bag to draw your heart away from being tender toward Jesus. Music. Sex. Money. Prestige.

We, as human beings, are the center of the whole controversy. We're here on *terra firma,* stuck behind enemy lines, with the devil using the rights of his domain, the world, to try to entice our flesh to respond to him and his temporal value system. We're dealing with the world, the flesh and the devil.

Jesus, however, taught about the distinction between darkness and light, life and death, foolishness and wisdom. There are no in-between regions. Since there are two kingdoms, we are relating either to Satan's destructive kingdom or to God's triumphant kingdom. This is the key to understanding what integrity is all about. *We are what we relate to.*

This principle is clearly illustrated in the way Peter responded to Jesus in Matthew 16. At this juncture I refer to what I wrote a few years ago in a booklet titled *The Doctrine of Fools:*[7]

> The sun was smoldering as [Jesus and his disciples] stood on the rocky shore of the Jordan River at Caesarea Philippi, a tiny village situated at the base of Mt. Hermon. Idols were nestled in the niches of a high rock wall dedicated to the Greek god, Pan. Jesus gazed intently into the eyes of each of His disciples. Amid the scene of rampant paganism, He powerfully welded the setting to His question, "But who do you say that I am?" After a moment of dramatic silence, Peter answered, "You are the Christ, the Son of the Living God." The Master immediately spoke, "You are blessed, Peter, because flesh and blood did not reveal it to you, but My Father which is in Heaven."
>
> . . . We can see in verse 16 of Matthew 16 that Peter is clearly relating to the kingdom of God. After Jesus blesses Peter, He commends him on the basis of the Source of the revelation. Jesus was excited because Peter was responding positively to the right kingdom.
>
> However, just seven verses later, we find Peter relating to the wrong kingdom. At this point Jesus has described His approaching suffering, death and resurrection. To this, Peter says rebukingly, "Oh no, you're not going to die. All these things won't happen to you."
>
> Here, Jesus once again deals with the one to whom Peter is relating. What a contrast! At this moment, Peter is responding to the wrong kingdom, because Jesus immediately says, "Get thee behind me, Satan . . ."
>
> In the first illustration, Peter is a wise man because of his heart response to God; however, he is a fool just moments later. Wisdom and foolishness have nothing to do with intelligence, social status or talent. Our wisdom or lack thereof is determined by the kingdom to which we relate.

When, like Peter, we relate to Satan's earth-bound power system, we actually are operating from a position of weakness. The cosmic sphere of influence betrays itself at every turn. When we are drawing our strength from the world system, we feel the need to puff ourselves up larger than life—like peacocks. Proud. Arrogant. Competitive. Tearing others down in order to build ourselves up. Envious of those who seem to "get away with it." Exaggerations. Lies. Rejoicing in iniquities. Searching for hidden meanings behind other people's actions. Slandering. Gossiping. Conniving. Constantly justifying personal behavior. Easily seduced if ego is inflated. Stirring up strife so that the outward environment matches the internal condition of our hearts. No empathy for suffering. Untrustworthiness. Demanding time and attention.

Because Satan's power system is a temporal provision based upon guilt, fear and manipulation, we face opposition and pressure without eternal values—hence disintegration (reduced to fragmented particles: mentally, emotionally, spiritually, physically and financially). The only way of escape is to exercise the personal freedom of choice.

We are relative beings. We are the *effect* of what we relate to, not the *cause* within ourselves. Everything ultimately boils down to a kingdom issue. Choosing to serve life or death.

When we choose to draw our resources from His system of authority and dominion, things are different. We are now operating from the position of strength. Humble. Merciful toward ourselves and others. Running without weariness. Walking the second mile without fainting. Willing to admit when wrong. Hospitable without grumbling behind closed doors. Letting others choose the best. Confident in the Lord. Turning the other cheek. Serving cheerfully. Giving liberally without demanding a return.

No defense mechanisms. Interested in *integration* on every level.

Jesus is our example of integrity. The fruit of His life is sweet. He voluntarily came to earth to be crucified in weakness. It took One who operated from the stance of strength to give His life for the sake of guilty, ungrateful people. You can't keep a resurrected man down!

Crucify Him. Stick Him in a tomb. Roll a huge stone over its mouth. Post guards. Three days later He's alive and well. You and I are in Christ, and that power is available to us. Think about it.

INtegrity, UPtegrity, OUTegrity

Meanwhile let's take a long hard look at three words that describe the scope of our subject in this chapter. I must warn you in advance, though, that a couple of these words won't be found in any dictionary; let's just call them "Freemanisms": UPtegrity, INtegrity and OUTegrity. These are not to be regarded as three separate character qualities. "UP" and "OUT" are components of "IN."

INtegrity has to do with internal experience: faithfulness and loyalty to truth; purpose is to glorify Jesus Christ and identify with His defeat over the devil; not dependent upon emotional support from others; able to think clearly and objectively under pressure; no fainting when confronted by trouble; final authority is the Word of God; inner poise when treated unfairly or criticized by others; clear conscience; boldness and courage under fire; a personal sense of destiny; untainted motives; honest relationship with the Holy Spirit; doing the details with dignity; no hidden agenda; sense of humor; studying the Bible; virtue; every chamber in the soul is filled with precious and pleasant riches.

As I look over the preceding list of qualities that

define *INtegrity,* I immediately think of Paul as he describes his internal motivation for living in 1 Thessalonians 2. He says that his ministry did not spring from error, from immorality or from craftiness. He refused to take advantage of people by lulling them into a false sense of security. His boldness for the Lord was not rooted in natural courage or bravado. He was a man who habitually, completely and repeatedly yielded his heart to Almighty God. His internal world was unsullied — free from hidden, personal motives rooted in selfishness.

UPtegrity has to do with our vertical relationship with God through His covenant of grace and mercy: trusting Him even when everything seems to be falling apart; accepting Him at His Word; heart inclined toward Him; worship performed unto the Lord — not to please or impress people; continual awareness that God is our audience; receiving His forgiveness after sinning; refusing to live in guilt; responding to His power after falling so that there is no repeated failure; keeping our heart's capacity always tender toward Jesus; realizing our individual relationship with God is based upon the fact that He initiated love first; believing God is faithful; zealously waging war in prayer because of the firm conviction that He listens and acts.

King David is the person who comes to mind when I think of *UPtegrity.* In the midst of all his failure he retained an absolute, childlike trust in a covenant-making, merciful God. Time and time again he cried out to Him. At one point, after arrogantly numbering the people in direct disobedience to God, he was given a choice. David could be judged directly by God or he could be judged by the people. David chose God's judgment. This reveals a heart that had confidence toward God and was willing to accept whatever God did without bitterness, resignation or additional backsliding, even if 70,000 people died as a result.

OUTegrity is the application of our vertical relation-

ship with God to horizontal relationships with people: a
promise made is a promise kept; admits when wrong —
doesn't blame, excuse or justify; never uses guilt or flattery
when trying to motivate others; returns a borrowed car
with a full tank of gas; lives to serve others and to give them
the advantage; a giver, not a taker; doesn't gossip or
slander; doesn't misrepresent facts; always seeks to re-
store; never plays the role of the professional victim, trying
to use shame or the silent treatment to manipulate someone who has caused emotional hurt.

When I think of *OUTegrity,* I picture a person coming out of his prayer closet. For an hour he has prayed. It's
been a wonderful time. He has felt so close to God.

He walks into the living room. In an abrasive tone,
his wife asks, "Where were you for the past hour?"

The warm feeling rapidly fades and is instantly
replaced with defensiveness and self-righteousness. "Well,
I was in my prayer closet — praying," he retorts icily.

Our praying friend has just been confronted with a
fascinating challenge. This is where the rubber meets the
road. OUTegrity is the practical expression of Christ to
those in our spheres of influence — even those who are un-
lovely. It is the outworking of INtegrity and UPtegrity.

How can we show our love for God? His answer
comes back loud and clear, "By laying your life down for
the people around you. The greatest among you is the servant of all. You exhibit your love for Me by the way you love
the brethren." That's a true disciple. That's a person with
integrity.

Keeping Perspective

Let me turn a corner rather sharply right here and
close out this chapter with a word of caution. Plain and
simple — it is so easy for us to lose sight of the person of

Christ and make a god out of the wonderful principle of integrity. Our human nature loves to distort the truth and live in idolatry.

Some venerate a particular day and forget the person. Some worship the ordinance of communion and miss the person. Some adore the principles of grace, love and doctrine but neglect the personality of the person of Christ in the process.

I saw a recent issue of the periodical *Times of Discovery*. On the front page, Martin De Haan alluded to this concept. He stated:

> In so many ways I give first-place honors to what is at best a second-place finisher.
> - My rationalism demands understanding.
> - My emotionalism craves feelings.
> - My activism prides itself in action.
> - My mysticism puts awareness before trust.
> - My legalism relies on rules.
> - My ritualism thirsts for the physical.
> - My traditionalism rests in the past.[8]

He said it so well. In the same breath we could have added *integrity* to that list: *My integrity breeds self-righteousness.*

And that's the way it is. Left to ourselves, we use our high personal standards as weapons to vilify, exclude or injure others who don't quite measure up. At best, we generate an air of impatience and bare tolerance. This becomes the breeding ground for cliques, schisms and hypocrisy.

The brand of integrity I desire to promote and export is that which flows from the head of the Church, Jesus Christ. It is rooted in the Word and is characterized by the fruit of the Holy Spirit: love, joy, peace, longsuffering, gentleness, goodness, faith, meekness, temperance.

Bert and Ferd love this brand of integrity.

Points to Ponder

1. What thoughts and emotions does the concept of spiritual warfare produce in your mind? If you could see a video of the battle, would you picture yourself as fighting hard, sitting on the sidelines or running away in the opposite direction?

2. Name one person you know who is an example of INtegrity, UPtegrity or OUTegrity. Have you ever seen him (or her) faced with a compromising situation? If so, what did he do?

3. What is the biblical definition of self-righteousness? How can you avoid it?

FOUR

Give Your Angel
a Break

*God always has an angel to help those
who are willing to do their duty.*
— *T. C. Cuysler*

This is international "Be Kind to Angels" week. You haven't heard about it? (I'm not surprised; I just invented it.)

I've been thinking about angels quite a lot lately. Come to think of it, I wonder what *they* think about? What do they talk about? Do they ever get bored protecting us? Do they have a sense of humor? Do they ever stand in front of us and make funny faces?

"Freeman, you're cracking up," you may say. "You keep talking like that and men in little white coats will come to take you away to a nice place with padded walls."

I know. I know. Please bear with me. I'm concerned for the angels. There are people who speak up for seals, whales and snails, yet no one speaks up for angels. I'm not sure why I have been chosen to speak on their behalf, but here I am, a frail voice crying in the wind.

Angels have a thankless job — protecting human beings. David made the observation in Psalm 34:7 that certain angels travel *everywhere* with people who claim respect for God. Read my lips — e-v-e-r-y-w-h-e-r-e.

Now, that can get pretty depressing. Bathrooms? Bedrooms? Speeding vehicles with radar detectors mounted on the dashboards? Hearing arguments, behind-closed-doors gossip and uncouth body noises during private moments? Being dragged to movies filled with four-letter words, violence and jiggling skin?

Take my angels for instance. (I'm an extremely active individual, so I figure I must have two of them.) I affectionately call them Bert and Ferd. (Finally, you get to meet them.) And I know they follow me everywhere.

Even though I've never seen them, I'm sure that when I get to heaven they'll show me videotapes of all the times they've intervened in potential car crashes, lightning storms and arguments with my wife. They're probably a good-natured, fun-loving couple of angelic beings. I wonder if they ever mimic me when I'm frustrated about something. "We're not laughing *at* you, we're laughing *with* you," they'd say.

Bert and Ferd put up with a lot from me. I hope they're not tired of me with my occasional mood swings, dull moments and brainstorms that turn out to be nothing more than slight drizzles.

I'm sure they're a dynamic duo, even though they've never personally communicated with me. At least, I've never heard them if they have. But I talk to them. Sometimes.

"Hey, Bert. Hey, Ferd. How are you doing? We've got a hectic day ahead of us, don't we? Mrs. Sledgepump is coming for counseling at 10 o'clock. Hmmm, my facial tissues are running low. And what about that pastors' luncheon at noon? Who wants to hear about broken air conditioning units and bargain prices on pew pads? You guys must get bored with some of the places I take you. Let's see, there are several more appointments this afternoon. And then Bible study tonight, with the nursery meeting right after. I can't wait! Oh, I almost forgot about those trash bags waiting in the garage. They have to be taken out to the end of the lane before collection time this afternoon. PU, the garage stinketh!"

I want to give my angels a break. They deserve it.

They love to worship God in His majestic presence. But I fall so short of ushering them into His presence.

They love holiness and absolute perfection. I desire both, but I have neither.

They love faith adventures and God-inspired enthusiasm. Even though I consider myself to be an up-beat, optimistic type of person, compared to what they're used to my soul is usually attracted to predictability, caution and security. I know what they want, but I can't consistently deliver.

How about you? Have you ever put yourself in an angel's position? How would you like to be assigned to yourself for twenty years? Or maybe fifty years? If you were an angel, would you have begged God for a transfer by now, asking to watch some spiritual saint who's stuck in solitary confinement somewhere in Siberia?

Get the picture? Angels have it rough. So why not work at giving your angel a break today?

You see, angels want to join in praise and adoration to the Father, yet the average human being probably doesn't pray more than ninety seconds a day. And that's your standard, dispassionate, grocery-list type petition at meal time.

Angels love to be around people who talk about their boss a lot, but most of us don't witness to others about Jesus. It's not because of the lack of instruction or the lack of opportunities. The number one reason why most Christians don't witness is because of the nagging realization that their personal lives aren't in line with biblical Christianity. Resident guilt feelings sap the long-term energy out of any motivation in the direction of witnessing. The common attitude is, "Who do I think I am? My own life isn't completely in order. And I'm going to tell someone else how to live his? You've got to be kidding!" Sounds so humble, doesn't it? The excuses of busyness, lack of education and fear are often really smokescreens for the real issue—lack of a clear conscience.

Angels love to be where the Scriptures are honored, yet personal Bible study and obedience to what has been studied is a rarity to say the least. It's sad, because angels are assigned to guard people who may be well-fed in terms of hearing sound teaching, but are starving when it comes to applying what has been heard. Angels must weep, if they can.

Many of us are so formal in both our private and public worship to Jesus. Angels don't want us to swing from chandeliers in an effort to liven things up, but how about a little more genuine enthusiasm? After all, there are some rather exciting things to consider. Can you imagine what it will be like when you arrive in heaven and see Jesus for the first time? I think that we'll be seeing some fairly reserved individuals making a mad dash in His direction and falling at His feet after giving Him a huge bear hug. Why not start practicing a little more freedom here on Earth so heaven won't be such a shock. You'll make your angel(s) very happy.

As the world's representative for angels' rights, I have now unburdened myself. Bert and Ferd must feel much better. They can rest easier at night, knowing that they have been assigned to such a fine spokesman.

Ahem . . . Now that the case for the vast angelic host has been presented, it's up to you. Are you going to start thinking of ways to minister to your guardian angel? Remember, it's "Be Kind to Angels" week. What a perfect time to start giving your angel a break.

Bert and Ferd are enjoying themselves, I think. They appreciate your support.

Points to Ponder

1. Answer the question asked in the chapter: If you were a guardian angel, how would you like to be assigned to yourself? What would be the toughest part of the job? Is there anything about you that would make you demand a transfer?

2. If you could *see* your guardian angel following you around, would you change any plans you have for this week? Would your lifestyle change significantly?

FIVE

Weasel
Clauses

*Even the wool he pulls over people's eyes
is 50% polyester.*
—Anonymous

When it comes to negotiating with legal contracts and high-powered attorneys, I am out of my league. When "lawyerese" language is used, I start asking questions. The *forthwiths*, *heretofores* and *henceforths* are words that cloud the meaning for me.

There is another thing that bothers me—the words and phrases hidden in all that legal mumbo jumbo that provide escape hatches from the contract for either party. Protection from the "what ifs?" is necessary for both parties, but what happens when an individual unwittingly signs a contract that is worded in such a way that it benefits only the other person? I guess that's why they say, "*Caveat Emptor*—let the buyer beware." And may I add, "*Caveat Vendor*—let the seller beware."

Our church owned ten acres of prime land in Columbia, Maryland. We were approached by a real estate speculator who offered us a contract to purchase the site.

49

My untrained eyes looked over the document with great interest. There were a few questionable parts, but on the whole I was impressed enough to ask our lawyer for his studied opinion.

After a few minutes spent perusing the document, he let out a lawyerly chuckle and said, "This is one of the more one-sided contracts I have ever seen." He then gave me a crash course in lawyerese, interpreting the hidden meanings behind each article in question. The contract was chock-full of loopholes, escape hatches and "weasel clauses"—all benefitting the buyer.

Our Contract With God

Weasel clauses. Whenever I think of them, I am reminded of my own propensity toward rationalization. There are more times than I'd care to admit when I've looked for an alternate route even though God's Word has specifically instructed me who to be and what to do. With weasel-like craft and stealth, I try to run from responsibility and discipline. During these moments I make feeble attempts at the art of negotiation with the Holy Spirit. Have you ever tried it? Let me tell you from personal experience—it doesn't work!

As humans we are constantly looking for what we believe to be the easy or better way out. The Lord invites us into a new area of maturity. Usually we accept His offer only after much scratching, screaming, kicking and biting. And usually it's only after we have exhausted all other alternatives.

Tough situations designed to mold, shape and mature us become our enemies. Pride motivates us to keep running—blaming and shaming, always pointing the finger at our circumstances ("I always have bad luck"), at others ("I was doing okay until he/she came into my life") or at

God ("He's against me. Every time I start enjoying life, He knocks me back down. I hope He's having fun").

These are all weasel clauses in our contract with God. Imagine if He allowed us to serve Him on our terms. Like spoiled brats we would threaten to backslide if He didn't make our wishes come true. We would threaten to call a unionized work stoppage if He ever treated us or anybody else "unfairly." We would defiantly try to abuse and intimidate Him at every turn.

Thank God that He is still in charge and that He doesn't meet our *perceived* needs! Instead, He knows our *real* needs and He meets us there every time. It usually isn't till much later that we look back on certain events in our life and see His hand in everything that happened.

The sooner we embrace this truth, the sooner we start taking responsibility for our actions. We stop the blame game. I'm reminded of a humorous article I once saw called "The Lighter Side of Kamikaze Pedestrians and Such":

> Accidents will happen. When they do, though, it's usually "the other guy's fault." Here are some telling remarks taken from actual insurance claim files:
> - "The other car collided with mine without giving warning of its intentions."
> - "An invisible car came out of nowhere, struck my vehicle and vanished."
> - "I'd been driving for forty years, when I fell asleep at the wheel and had an accident."
> - "A pedestrian hit me and went under my car."
> - "Coming home, I drove into the wrong house and collided with a tree I don't have."
> - "As I approached the intersection, a sign suddenly appeared in a place where no sign had ever been before. So I was unable to stop in time to avoid an accident."
> - "The pedestrian had no idea which direction to run,

so I ran over him."

- "The telephone pole was approaching. I was attempting to swerve out of the way when it struck my front end."
- "I pulled away from the side of the road, glanced at my mother-in-law and headed over the embankment."
- "As I reached the intersection, a hedge sprang up, obscuring my vision. I just didn't see the other car."
- "The guy was all over the road, and I had to swerve a number of times before hitting him."
- "My car was legally parked when it backed into the other vehicle."[1]

Between snorts and giggles, I realize that some of the preceding excuses are the result of classic miscommunication. Yet they all still reveal the human propensity toward rationalization. It's kind of like this brief encounter between two major players in our internal worlds:

Pride and Memory had a disagreement. Memory said, "This is the way it happened."

"No it didn't," retorted Pride.

"Okay," Memory said meekly.[2]

The Fine Art of "Editing"

Rationalization: Highly systemized and intricate thought patterns, one leading logically to the next, that assist a person in avoiding clear-cut, unwavering obedience to specific mandates, such as that of the Bible: "I've always been like that. I guess I'll never change"; "Oh, that's just me"; "I can't help it . . . I'm human." Such excuses encourage one to diminish or completely ignore the Holy Spirit's work of conviction; they also shave the edge off disobedience.

Think of how a motion picture is made. After millions of dollars are spent to shoot several hundred minutes of film, the tough work begins — editing. A group of people decide which scenes to alter or cut in order to produce a movie that will be a smash hit at the box office.

Rationalization works in a similar vein. The PR image we present to God and others is, in many ways, a finely edited production. We expend great amounts of energy editing certain ugly scenes in our memory or trying to cut out some of the negative characteristics of our personalities. We then splice the film back together again without confronting the underlying issues that caused those scenes to occur in the first place. Pride is the editor.

There are a number of scenes that I would have liked to edit out of my life. Like the hunting license incident. And many other occasions when I have come too close to yielding to temptation or actually given in.

The Yabbit Club

Because of these incidents I have come to realize there is no such thing as being taken by surprise when it comes to evil. *"Yeah, but it happened so suddenly." "Yeah, but I was vulnerable and after thinking about it for a few moments everything seemed to be okay." "Yeah, but after all, it's my body; I wasn't hurting anybody else."* I was a long-standing, charter member of the Yabbit (Yeah, but . . .) Club.

Under the searchlight of truth in God's Word and the conviction of the Holy Spirit, all of my "logical" reasons sounded so hollow when I came eyeball to eyeball with the reality that my heart had been cold toward eternal things for months prior to giving in to temptation. My deviation from the straight and narrow wasn't a sudden incident without warning. Religious activity and good works had been a substitute for inner tenderness, passionate prayer and holy zeal. Everything had looked fine and functional on the outside to the casual observer, but on the inside the attraction to temptation was brewing. I was ten miles wide and only three inches deep. I was an accident looking for a place to happen.

Someone once defined an *excuse* as the skin of the reason stuffed with lies. (Kind of like a hot dog . . . think about it!) Seriously, the preceding definition is absolutely true. Any time I feel the irresistible urge to justify, explain, defend or excuse my actions, I am learning to pause a moment and ask myself the following questions: *Will Jesus Christ accept this explanation when I stand before Him at the Bema Seat Judgment? Will this situation be a significant issue 1000 years from now?* I usually shut up.

Stay the Course

There is a verse that has helped me cut the weasel clauses out of my relationship with God. Read it carefully: ". . . receive with meekness the engrafted word, which is able to save [correct] your souls" (James 1:21*b*).

This Scripture became especially precious to me a number of years ago when I visited a 300-ton ship. It had been purchased by a gallant group of people from many churches for the purpose of performing interministerial work in the Caribbean Basin. A previously unseasoned crew had brought the 118-foot vessel on a sometimes harrowing voyage from Norway to the United States. They had come by way of the unpredictable North Atlantic under the guidance of a veteran Swedish sea captain.

While touring the ship, I stopped off at the navigation room, a tiny cubicle within sight of the giant steering wheel. The gracious skipper was there. "Is this vessel classified as a boat or as a ship?" I inquired after a brief introduction.

He paused and thought for a moment. "Vell, ven she

is in port, she is ship, but ven she is in middle of ocean, she is boat," he said with a heavy accent and a chuckle.

I looked up at a map of the Atlantic Ocean tacked to the wall and noticed a crudely penciled path from Stavanger, Norway, to Baltimore, Maryland. I was intrigued by the X marks placed erratically along the line. In some places, the line was fairly straight and the X marks were several inches apart. But in other places, like on the west side of the Azores Islands, the X marks were bunched closely together and the line zigzagged dramatically.

In talking with the captain, I discovered that the white-haired mariner was from the old school. He didn't like to use the new-fangled, computerized navigational equipment. Give him a map, a sextant and a compass along with the sun and the stars and he was happy. The X's were marked every time a sighting had been taken. And those sightings were crucial, particularly during a storm. They had been blown off course a number of times as indicated by the sometimes squiggly path.

Many moons have passed since that experience, yet to this day I cannot get away from an analogy that came to me. What I witnessed in that midget-sized compartment is an amazingly accurate story of what happens in our lives.

You and I are like that vessel. It doesn't take much to blow us off course. That is why we need to have objective assistance. God's Word is continually available to correct our position. Certain Scriptures determine longitude while other verses ascertain the latitudinal degree of our spiritual location.

A fraction of a degree off course is imperceptible to the human conscience, but after a few months pass the true motives of the heart become obvious. A good conscience can become a defiled conscience which later becomes a seared conscience. It is possible to get to such a low point in our lives that sin doesn't bother us anymore. This, of course, leads to an evil conscience.

It all begins with our natural desire to learn about evil. God wants us to have inquisitive minds, but with evil it is different. He wants us to know evil, *not* by experience but by developing a categorical understanding from the Bible on that particular subject. Once we understand God's view, anything less than His truth will stick out like a sore thumb.

If, however, we meddle with evil we are soon seduced by our own lusts and our attention is focused on sensual fulfillment. At this point, in much the same way that Eve questioned the word of God when Lucifer tempted her in the Garden of Eden, we also begin to foolishly question instruction based upon Scripture. Little by little, like a lost ship at sea, we drift from the straight and narrow course.

As the carnal, sensual focus continues, our unrestrained lust becomes pregnant with need and brings forth sin. Our conscience becomes violated by the act of sin, and suddenly we are stirred with wretched guilt.

Since our emotional system wasn't designed to bear the pressure of guilt, we respond in one of three ways:

1. We can try to rationalize away the guilt while continuing in sin.

2. We can try to earn brownie points from God by doing good deeds to compensate for the sin.

3. We can confess our sin and experience God's forgiveness through the blood of Jesus Christ.

This is a crucial point of decision for us. Either we run from the light through an elaborate system of rationalization or we run boldly to the Throne of Grace. What we do with the guilt determines whether or not we lose our bearings. The greatest way to correct the direction of our souls is to receive, with meekness, the Word of God.

Grafting the Word

Concord apples on a Mackintosh apple tree? Is it possible? Yes, by grafting a healthy branch from a Concord tree into the trunk of a Mackintosh tree.

Can a weak-willed human being actually experience love, forgiveness and a practical victory over sin? Yes, by meditating upon the Word.

Here's how it works. Are you having a problem with sensual lust? Memorize and personalize Romans 6 – 8. Live with these three chapters day and night. Meditate upon the principles found in them while eating, working, daydreaming, showering, walking and driving. Meanwhile, ask the Holy Spirit to pump reality and joy into what you are pondering. Watch what happens after one year. You'll be amazed at the transformation that will have taken place. A renewed mind.

"But what if I get blown off course?" you may ask. Once again — the negative trends of our souls can be corrected by receiving with meekness what the Word of God has to say about forgiveness. The Emergency Room of the Bible is 1 John 1:9, "If we confess our sins, He is faithful and just to forgive us our sins and to cleanse us from all unrighteousness." What seems to be so *simple* is actually *profound*. What seems to be so *profound* is actually *simple*.

Sharon learned the hard way. She had happened to listen one afternoon to the radio talk show I was hosting on WABS in the Washington, D.C., area a few years ago. If my memory serves me correctly, the question of divorce had been raised on the program and my comments had included a list of some rather shocking statistics enumerating the negative effects that divorce has upon children, finances,

emotions, etc. I had stated that the energy needed to spare
a rocky marriage was less costly than the long-term heartache experienced on every level after the fact of divorce.

As soon as the program ended, my producer came
into the studio with a message stating that I had a
telephone call to return. I should have noticed that she
rolled her eyes while handing me the note.

I was not prepared for the verbal assault. After brief
introductions, Sharon lit into me. "Who do you think you
are? I am outraged by your response to that question about
divorce."

Knowing how carefully I had answered the question
on the air, I immediately thought either she had not heard
my entire response or she was suffering from extreme guilt
because of a personal decision regarding divorce. I soon discovered the latter to be true.

I allowed her to fuss and fume at me for a few
minutes and then I began to ask questions to gently probe
what really was happening. Slowly but surely the picture
was painted. Raised in a Christian home with strong moral
values. Married for sixteen years to a very successful
businessman. Four children ranging from eight to fifteen
years of age. High profile involvement in a local church.
Marriage falling apart. Madly in love with a single man she
had worked with during a church function. Secret meetings. Adultery. Seriously considering divorce. Tantalizing
prospect of remarriage. Geographical change. Presto-chan-
go. A new life!

It all was so neat and clean. No jagged edges in her
mind. Her reasons for every decision were so logical. She
was willing to give up her marriage and her kids. Every
theological impediment had been dealt with — in her way of
thinking, anyway.

Sharon was deceived. There is no other way to put

it. Her mind was made up and she didn't want to be confused by facts. The ship of her life was dangerously off
course, with a full head of steam—headed toward the rocks.
If I could have seen a copy of her commitment to God, it
would have been chock-full of caveats, loopholes, escape
hatches and weasel clauses. Her motto was: *God has not
called me to be holy. Rather, He has called me to be happy—
on my terms. Period.*

I respect the validity and therapeutic value of counseling techniques such as open-ended questions and
reflection of emotion, but after dialoging with Sharon for
over thirty minutes, I discerned that those counseling techniques alone wouldn't cut to the root issue. The cold, hard
realities of truth from God's Word were needed. Our conversation was a precious window of opportunity for Satan
to be exposed and defeated.

I was uncharacteristically blunt. Drawing from my
counseling experience and theological studies, I described
the underlying issues that she was grappling with.

I gave her an action plan which included the reading of a book about the anatomy of adultery, the study of
certain Scriptures, marriage counseling, repentance and
breaking off all contact with her lover. To my surprise, she
listened. We closed in prayer. But she made no promises.

A month ago, I received a surprise phone call from
Sharon. Guess what! She is still married to her
businessman husband (she loves him dearly). She is still
with their four children (the oldest just graduated from
high school). They still go to the same church (her former
lover received a career promotion to Arizona not long after
our conversation).

I respect Sharon. It took a lot of guts for her to confront the unrealistic expectations, unresolved guilt,
juvenile fantasies and selfishness that she had embraced

for years. She was willing to submit to the Scriptures as her final authority. She deleted the weasel clauses in her relationship with God and in her marriage.

I'm sure that the process was longer, harder and messier than she had previously anticipated. But after remembering our prior conversation and after hearing the refreshingly different sparkle in her voice in this conversation, I could tell that she felt it was all worthwhile.

Her new motto is: *God has not called me to be happy. Rather, He has called me to be holy.* But do you want to know something? She would say, "Doing it God's way is much more fun than trying to live life my way. And I'm having a blast!"

And Bert and Ferd are rejoicing, I'm sure.

Points to Ponder

1. Have you written a few weasel clauses into your contract with God? What are they? How can you delete them?

2. Can you think of a time when you've rationalized your way out of a situation where you should have obeyed God? Imagine that the exact same circumstance will unfold tomorrow. Write a new "script" for yourself, using the Word of God as your compass to chart your course of action.

SIX

The Power of a Squeaky Clean Conscience

*The serene, silent beauty of a holy life
is the most powerful influence in the world,
next to the might of God.*
— Blaise Pascal

Married professional man, 47, with problems in home life seeks dalliance with a married/unmarried intelligent woman.

They were curious about who responds to personal ads and why, so the folks at the *Bottom Line* newsletter decided to place the above ad in two major publications just to see what would happen.[1] The response was overwhelming. Among them . . .

- I am a thirty-four-year-old female — pretty, Rubenesque, brown hair, dark blue eyes. I work as a nurse in a large urban hospital. My friends consider me bright, honest, interesting, conservatively Bohemian, sensitive and sensual. I have the usual vices.

- I am interested in the same things you are. I'm thirty-six, married. Discretion is very important to me. Please call only between 9 A.M. and 4:30 P.M.

- I'm a forty-two-year-old female seeking a sensitive, caring man for a relationship in which friendship is key. I want to share thoughts, laughter, hugs and togetherness with you.

- At forty-seven you're at a great age — young enough to be sexy and upbeat, yet mature enough to appreciate me . . . I don't have the energy for a demanding full-time affair, so your marriage is actually a plus for me. I always avoid the bar scene, but love and lust are what I need.

- Welcome to the club! I'm thirty-six, married, a professional in the advertising business. Home is not exactly a nest I look forward to flying back to tonight. We might share a few things! Write me!

- I can "dally" during the day or evening. Please don't let my answering machine put you off.

- I'm intelligent and married. I live in a deeply wooded area along a river where deer are an everyday occurrence . . . I could see you during the week but never on weekends. I'm tall, slim and decent-looking. You could be seen with me without shame.

- Like you, I am married and seeking an attractive, sincere friend to add new joys and laughter to my life. I am a very pretty, tall, forty-five-years-young redhead who is bright, charming, very warm and lots of fun to be with. I am definitely not a swinger . . . I can't give you a phone number because I have a young daughter at home . . . Let's see if we have anything in common.

- Well, here I am — bright, attractive, very much married, and very much in need of a joyful, discreet afternoon dalliance. We have a lot in common. I work at home, and it is best to call in the morning. If you get my answering machine, please do not leave a message — I'm sure you understand. Looking forward to meeting you.

Wow! These women are uninhibited and free. They know what they want and they are getting it. Nothing seems to stand in their way. They are liberated and unrestrained in their pursuit of happiness. Aren't they?

Something seems to be raining on their parades. In many of these short responses, there is a note of hesitancy. I catch occasional hints of the conscience at work.

"I can't give you my phone number because I have a young daughter at home." (I wonder why?)

"I'm thirty-six and married. Discretion is very important to me. Please call me only between 9 A.M. and 4:30 P.M." (*Hmmm* . . . I stroke my chin and strike a thoughtful pose on that one.)

"If you get my answering machine, please do not leave a message—I'm sure you understand." (Very interesting.)

C'mon, Conscience, why can't you leave these poor women alone? They all seem to have their reasons for answering such an ad. They just want a little excitement. It's their lives and they're big girls now. They're not hurting anybody, are they? Please stop pestering them.

The Conscience—Man's Best Friend

The conscience. It never takes a rest. With an ever-sweeping spotlight, it diligently stands guard over our internal worlds, identifying every alien thought or desire. No enforcement. No interpretations. Just whistle blowing.

Like a contentious spouse it seems to nitpick all the time. You cannot escape its scrutiny. You can stomp around like an enraged rhinoceros, but it will not get intimidated. You may defile it or harden it, causing it to malfunction, but it will always stick around. That's not a threat—it's a promise.

At the outset, let's get something straight. The conscience is our best friend. What is the conscience, though, and how does it operate? Well, in Romans 2:14,15, the apostle Paul likened it to the judge, jury and witness in a courtroom. None of those people make up new laws. They merely apply and bear witness to the laws that have already been passed.

In other words, when you stop your car on a busy street and help someone change their flat tire, your conscience gets excited and says, "All right! Good job! Keep it up!" It approves of your actions and you experience warm, fuzzy feelings all over. It didn't devise the "it's-nice-to-help-change-a-flat-tire" rule.

If, however, you stop your car, get out, walk over and steal the other fellow's spare tire just before he puts it on, your conscience says, "Now, that was wrong! Stop what you are doing right now and return that tire!" The conscience didn't design the "don't-steal-a-tire" law either. It merely disapproves of your actions and you immediately feel the "guilties."

The Window of the Soul

In Matthew 6:22,23, Jesus compared the conscience to an inner window He called the eye. Now, there are a couple of things about windows that intrigue me. The World Window Washing Association (WWWA) is happy about the first one: Windows get dirty.

I don't know about you, but I enjoy the feeling of satisfaction that courses through my body when I clean my car windshield. Birds happen to love my parked car. They sit in the trees and drop precious little deposits that streak right down the driver's side of the windshield. I spray glass cleaner, get out my paper towel and indulge myself with that beguiling, high-pitched "ee-oo-ee-oo-ee-oo" sound. Ah, it's clean!

A second fact about windows is that they do not produce light. Clean windows merely allow free passage of light that is already shining.

Imagine yourself lying on your bed, reading the Bible by the light of the noonday sun. You are receiving inspiration, wisdom and inner guidance from what you are learning. Without your noticing, a slight film begins to form on the only window in your bedroom. Gradually, the room becomes darker as the window gets dirtier. You squint your eyes, propping the Bible up in an effort to see more clearly. Before long the window is absolutely filthy. You can't see a thing in the darkness.

This is what happens to the window called the conscience. If our conscience is squeaky clean, it will permit God's full light to penetrate our souls with inner direction and power. But every time the conscience is violated by sin, the window gets dirtier until we have sinned so much that it is completely dirty and no light can come through.

I am often amazed at how seemingly fervent Christians can backslide so dramatically. I understand the spiritual principles involved, but what shocks me is the intensity with which evil is pursued. People who are spiritually riding high one moment find themselves entangled in sin's deceitful web the next.

There is a young man, twenty-one, who comes to mind. He experienced a wonderful conversion to Jesus Christ. The transformation was remarkable. He left a life of sex, drugs, crime—you name it. For seven months he was on-fire for God. All of a sudden, it seemed, he turned the other way.

My heart is sad. I've gone to see him. I've written him. I pray for him daily. I have seen no results yet. I do believe, though, that the Word of God does not return void.

Recently I saw one of his drug-addict friends on the street and this is what he said: "Hey man, I don't know about Ed. I'm scared. He's worse than he ever was before. I liked him better before. Last Sunday, in fact, I even tried to get him to come to church with me. He refused."

This is a prime example of an evil conscience at work. Ed is no longer guided by the norms and standards of the Scripture. He is only happy and comfortable with the dark side.

The conscience is tough in terms of convicting us of wrong and yet at the same time it is fragile. It can be forced to malfunction if we add sin to sin without repentance. Therefore, we must be careful how we treat our consciences.

Helping Your Conscience

Around the time that I started writing this book, noted author and lecturer Warren Wiersbe found out about the theme I was tackling and he graciously sent me a copy of his book *Meet Your Conscience*. He hoped it would be of some help to me. Of some help? I practically devoured it! His writings have influenced me greatly. And with his permission I have extensively borrowed ideas from his work for this next section.[2]

Your conscience is important. It is vital that you read the *Manufacturers Handbook* to learn about its upkeep and maintenance. If you follow directions, it will serve you marvelously during your lifetime. Let's take a look at why your conscience is so important.

1. Conscience is God's Gift

Some say that the conscience comes *from behind us* — it's a part of evolution. As man evolved over the centuries, conscience evolved within him. In *The Descent of*

Man Darwin writes, "Of all the differences between man and the lower animals, the moral sense, or conscience, is by far the most important." Yet Darwin couldn't explain the origin of the conscience.

Others say that it comes *from around us:* The conscience is merely the sum total of all the standards of society. Society does help to give us standards, but society does not give us the conscience. While people have different customs and standards in different parts of the world, conscience still functions the same no matter where you go.

Still others say that conscience comes *from within us.* Many psychiatrists want us to believe that we have manufactured our own conscience — it's the by-product of the way Mother raised us and Father disciplined us.

I disagree with these explanations. According to the Word of God, conscience came *from above us.* Conscience is a universal phenomenon; therefore, it must have a common source, and that source is God.

2. Conscience Guides Our Conduct

I've heard people say, "Let your conscience be your guide," and to some degree this is good advice. In Acts 24:16, Paul admitted that his conscience needed exercise. If the conscience is not exercised, it will begin to function in the wrong way.

The Holy Spirit uses the Word of God to show us the will of God, and the conscience is involved in the process. If your conscience is functioning the way it should, then you have a compass to direct you, a light to guide you and a law to give you wisdom in the Christian life.

First Timothy 1:19 says that when you start playing around with your conscience, you're heading for shipwreck. When you don't follow the compass or try to change it, you're going to run aground.

3. Conscience Strengthens for Service

We read in 1 Timothy 1:5 that the purpose of the ministry of the Word of God is that we might love from a pure heart, have a good conscience and have sincere faith that is not hypocritical.

In his ministry Paul was very careful to have a clear conscience and to minister to the consciences of others.

4. Conscience Strengthens Fellowship

Romans 14 and 15 and 1 Corinthians 8, 9 and 10 show that some people have strong consciences and some have weak consciences.

Those with a weak conscience often create problems in the fellowship. They lack knowledge, are easily wounded and offended, are unstable, tend to be critical of others, are legalistic and have confused priorities. What causes this? I think basically these people are afraid of freedom.

The people with a strong conscience possess spiritual knowledge, have discernment, enjoy their freedom in Christ and are tolerant of differences in others. Their responsibilities include graciously receiving the weak, refraining from arguing or causing the weak to stumble, and making peace.

You want to become the kind of Christian who has a strong conscience that has grown through love, truth from God's Word and spiritual exercises. Claim and enjoy the privileges and freedoms we have in Christ, but never use them to hurt others. A pure conscience strengthens our fellowship.

5. Conscience Encourages Witnessing

When your conscience is right between you and God, it makes little difference what people say about you or do to you. You're free to speak about the One who transformed your life and made you a new person.

Nothing will keep your mouth shut like a conscience that convicts you. When we know we've done something wrong, when there's something between us and the Lord, we're not very good witnesses!

6. Conscience Helps in Prayer

When I kneel to pray, if my conscience convicts me, I have to get the matter straightened out before I can talk to God. It's wonderful to be able to pray in the will of God and not be accused by our consciences. Then we can pray effectively.

7. Conscience Affects Citizenship

Romans 13:1 makes it clear that God has established government: ". . . the powers that be are ordained of God." In light of this, is civil disobedience valid?

There are several instances in Scripture where people disobeyed man's law when it contradicted God's higher law. If your conscience is functioning as it should, it helps you know when to obey and when not to obey the law.

Be sure, though, that your conscience controls all aspects of your citizenship and not just areas you feel like letting it control. I read about university students who refuse to go into the army because of conscience, but their conscience doesn't bother them when they get drunk or when they wreck an automobile at high speed or when they cheat on examinations. I have a hard time believing a person is conscientious about war when he is not conscientious about anything else.

Suppose you are told not to witness? Suppose, like Daniel, you are told not to pray? Suppose, like the Hebrew midwives during Moses' time, you are told to murder babies? What will you do? A good conscience helps us to be good citizens and to use our citizenship to the glory of God.

8. Conscience Helps Build Character

If you do not use your faculties, they become useless. If a person ties his right arm to his body and doesn't use it, it will atrophy.

Our spiritual senses function in a similar way. If we don't exercise our spiritual sense, then we never learn how to discern between good and evil. It is important for us to build up our conscience — to have a good conscience, a pure conscience, a conscience void of offense — because this helps us to build Christian character.

We've just discovered eight benefits that show the importance and power of a clear conscience. But how can we develop and maintain a squeaky clean conscience?

Steps to Cleaning the Conscience

First we need to ask ourselves some tough questions: Are we playing around with a particular sin, like a moth trying to fly as close as it can to the flame without being burned? Are we engaging in shallow repentance, making excuses to people and to God instead of confessing our sin? Are we attempting to convince ourselves that there is a measurable difference between big sins and little sins? Are we more concerned about our reputation before people than our character before God?

An affirmative answer to any one of the preceding questions should set off an alarm. The inner window of the conscience is badly smudged. Quite frankly, it desperately needs cleaning because we have been flirting with what the Scripture calls an evil conscience.

As we saw in the last chapter, an evil conscience develops over a period of time. That is why the initial step for us to develop a clean conscience is to allow the Holy

Spirit to penetrate our hearts with searching, probing questions from the Word.

The second step is to quickly agree with the Holy Spirit's estimate and evaluation of our spiritual condition. By doing so, we are kept from grieving, quenching or resisting Him. What a freedom!

There's a big difference between the Holy Spirit's conviction and Satan's condemnation. Satan accuses repeatedly, leaving you with a sense of hopelessness and despair. The Holy Spirit, on the other hand, convicts but immediately shows the way of escape. He points to what Jesus did on Calvary as a once-and-for-all finished work.

This brings us to the third step. After agreeing with His estimation of the dirty condition of our inner window, we immediately agree with what Christ did about it—dying on the cross.

First John 1:9 says we can confess our sins. When we do, He is faithful and just to forgive our sins and to cleanse us from *all* unrighteousness. Now, that's exciting! The Greek term used in this verse for *confess* is *homologeo* which literally means to agree with God. Get the picture? We agree that we were off course and then we agree with what Christ has done about it some 2,000 years ago. Our fellowship is renewed and Satan is defeated! It's that simple.

Here comes the real challenge. Step number four is to actually believe that we have been forgiven. Remember when I told the lie about my hunting license? After I had asked for forgiveness, I lived under the weight of guilt for months. As I compare the truth from God's Word to my experience during those months, I clearly see that I engaged in the foolish practice of beating myself up with condemnation.

Actually my guilt was the result of disguised pride.

Under the covering of false humility, I was arrogantly claiming that my sin was too big and too much for Christ to forgive. Therefore, I had to personally hound myself with a ton of "why" questions.

Pride refuses to experience total forgiveness. True humility not only accepts mercy, but also gives it away — freely. In the past I have been a sucker for guilt. But not anymore. It's not for me!

Oh, yes, I'll accept a momentary flash of real guilt from the Holy Spirit when I sin. However, if Satan projects pseudo-guilt, I ignore him. He can go play in the traffic. I refuse to call my travel agent and book a "guilt trip."

We've now arrived at the fifth and final step to developing a clear conscience. We must continue to keep short accounts with the Holy Spirit through habitual intake of the Word of God. This causes us to maintain an open, honest relationship with the Holy Spirit and keeps the inner window of the conscience sparkling clean.

I would recommend the purchase of a complete concordance of the Bible. Inhale the Scripture by meditating upon specific verses that bring inner stability. What are you struggling with the most? Is it fear, guilt, lust or bitterness? Identify a felt need and start there. Then, if your heart begins to condemn you, encourage yourself with the Word. It's a long and sometimes difficult process, but it works. The Bible has the uncanny ability to transform a person with a weak conscience into someone with a strong one.

The squeaky clean conscience allows the light of godly authority to shine through. You can look the devil in the eye — and spit. You can see the allurement of the world — and walk away. You can feel the temptation of your flesh — and worship God.

This kind of stuff makes Bert and Ferd jump for joy.

Points to Ponder

1. Which of the eight characteristics of a good conscience is most compelling to you right now? Why?

2. Think of a time when you experienced guilt or condemnation over something you did (or didn't do). Now, think of a time when you felt God's firm, loving conviction about some sin instead. Did you respond differently to it? If not, why?

SEVEN

Rock of Jell-O

*God will not cheat you from something
that will make you unutterably weak.*
—Anonymous

Jell-O. A friend of mine calls it "nervous pudding." In its
liquid state, it can be poured into a mold. When the
gelatin becomes firm, it can be served. If the dish is tapped
or the table is bumped, it quivers and jiggles, yet it retains
its original shape.

We are kind of like Jell-O. On the one hand, we are
fragile beings—always one hair's breadth away from insanity. While on the other hand, we are a stubborn,
rebellious bunch.

We pump ourselves up every day to fit into the
world's mold. Coffee. Shower. Deodorant. Hairspray.
Cologne. We strive to win through intimidation. Confidence seems to ooze out of our every pore. We attempt to
project an I've-got-it-all-together image.

Our inner world is another story. It is characterized
by second-guessing, insecurity, roller-coaster emotions. We
are scared little boys and girls in a dog-eat-dog, "adult"
society, trying to bump through life without sustaining too
many psychic blows to our self-worth.

All of us experience this dichotomy in varying degrees of intensity. We endeavor to maintain a fine-line balance—and a precarious balance it is. A heart attack, a business reversal or some other crisis can change our priorities and our entire outlook on life instantly.

We're like Jell-O—shaking and quaking our way through life. When we put confidence in our human talent, ability, knowledge or experience, we are setting ourselves up for trouble. Any circumstance that hits 9.3 on the Richter scale can send us quivering and jiggling into the next decade as emotional wrecks—hiding behind masks of strength and security. We need a support system that goes far beyond what we can touch, taste, see, hear or smell.

The Source of Our Support System

There's a vital key to the successful Christian walk that's often overlooked: *the fear of the Lord*. Without it we suffer through life tolerating self-pity, a lack of integrity, a tendency to rationalize and an evil conscience. With it we become special treasures to God, lead satisfying lives and avoid oceans of troubles. The choice is ours.

Before going too much further, let's get something straight about fearing the Lord. I'm not talking about a fear that produces torment and bondage. Such dread has no lasting moral effect. It may provide the momentary impetus needed to make one walk right, talk right, dress right and smell right for a while, but it cannot restrain human depravity for long.

The fear I'm talking about is something quite different. Consider this example: I fear electrical power lines. I don't, however, lie awake at night with *Friday-the-13th-Part-VII* panic in my eyes, terrorized by the thought of the awesome potential of electricity to maim, kill and destroy. Instead, whenever clicking on the overhead lights, turning on the radio or taking a hot shower, I enjoy the provision of electricity that was transported to my home via the power lines. I have great respect for them: I'm not about to go outside right now, lean an aluminum extension ladder against the lines, climb up and hit them repeatedly with an axe. No way!!

Get the picture? The fear of the Lord is a fear without torment, yet at the same time it is a reverential awe. We trust the Lord and enjoy His moment-by-moment provision.

That definition is missing a key ingredient, though. It fails to address the power and significance behind the fear of the Lord.

Here's a more complete definition of the fear of the Lord: *The continual awareness that I am in the presence of a holy, just and almighty God, and that every thought, word, action and deed is open before Him and is being judged by Him.*[1]

Just think. If you lived with the daily reality that God is scrutinizing everything you do, think and say, and that some day you will stand before Him, how do you think it would affect your current lifestyle? How would it affect the content of your conversations? What attitudes would be corrected? This is where the rubber meets the road.

The Many Faces of Fear

As finite beings, we're going to shake and quake anyway, so we may as well tremble in His presence, acknowledging our frailty, ripping off our masks and receiving His strength. It's the only reasonable way to live!

There are certain things we can do to learn the fear of the Lord. One of those is to grasp the intent of the words used in the original languages to describe the various aspects of fear, and discover how they apply to the fear of the Lord.

The Hebrew root for *fear* is *yârê*.[2] It means, "to frighten, to revere, to affright, be [made] afraid, to dread." Let's take a peak at some of the words that will assist us in adopting a practical understanding and application of the fear of the Lord in our everyday lives.

Trembling

Webster says that the act of trembling is "a fit or spell of involuntary shaking or quivering; the vibratory movement of shivering or shuddering."[3]

A graphic example in the Old Testament of trembling occurred when the mighty King Belshazzar saw a huge hand miraculously appear, crashing his party and etching some threatening words on the wall. "Then the king's countenance was changed, and his thoughts troubled him, so that the joints of his loins were loosed, and his knees smote one against another . . . and his lords were [astonished]" (Daniel 5:6-9).

Another lively illustration of trembling is the description of how the Roman guards reacted to the angel that bounced the huge stone away from the mouth of Jesus' tomb. "His appearance was like lightning, and his clothes were white as snow. The guards were so afraid that they trembled and became as dead men" (Matthew 28:3,4, TEV).

Astonishment

The Hebrew word *shâmêm*[4] means "to stun, to stupefy, to devastate, to grow numb in the state of bewilderment." When confronted by an awesome event, the individual who is astonished experiences the inability to talk.

This word comes from the Latin term *extonare*.[5] *Ex* means "out" and *tonare* means "to thunder." Have you ever been "thunderstruck" or "struck dumb"?

Paul encountered a "minor distraction" while on his way to persecute Christians in Damascus. Suddenly a light from the sky flashed around him. He was thrown to the ground and hit the dust as a dead man. Paul could barely squeak out the question, "Who are you, Lord?" His traveling companions were speechless as they took in the whole scene.

The prophet Zechariah said, "Be silent, everyone, in the presence of the LORD, for his is coming from his holy dwelling place" (Zechariah 2:13, TEV). King Solomon's counsel must also be heeded: "Guard your steps when you go to the house of God. Go near to listen . . . Do not be quick with your mouth, do not be hasty in your heart to utter anything before God. God is in heaven and you are on the earth, so let your words be few" (Ecclesiastes 5:1,2, NIV).

Fright

Fright can be defined as a fear caused by sudden danger. The Greek term *ekthambeo*[6] literally means "to shrink or shiver with fear." This violent reaction is usually temporary and of short duration.

The semi-seaworthy disciples experienced this type of fear while riding out an unexpected storm on the Sea of Galilee. After being rudely awakened from a pleasant slumber, Jesus stilled the boisterous waves with an authoritative rebuke. The already jittery disciples became increasingly frightened, exclaiming, "Who is this? Even the wind and waves obey him!" (Mark 4:41, NIV)

A couple of years later, these same disciples huddled in a room to discuss the odds of the resurrection of their Messiah. Without warning, Jesus appeared and said, "Peace be with you." They were startled and frightened, thinking they had just seen a ghost.

Dread

Webster defines dread as "an anticipatory apprehension of impending doom or danger." One word in the original Hebrew language, *pâchad*,[7] describes it as being "startled by sudden alarm" and being "made to shake." Dread is felt when one is experiencing an intense restlessness while expecting agony, loss or some other type of personal injury to occur. Dread maintains the high adrenalin level for a longer period of time than that of *fright*.

Near the beginning of his ministry, Isaiah was warned by God: "Do not join in the schemes of the people and do not be afraid of the things they fear [dread]. Remember that I, the LORD Almighty, am holy; I am the one you must fear [dread]" (Isaiah 8:12,13, TEV).

God and His display of authority instilled such an awe in Isaiah that he never wanted to experience the sure-fire judgment of God which comes as the result of personal sin. However, if we are walking in obedience, we enjoy an optimistic outlook on life and never have to dread what He might do to us. What freedom!

A prime example of this was illustrated in a volume from the Institute in Basic Youth Conflicts:

> Job stated of God, "Shall not his excellence make you afraid? And his dread fall upon you?" (Job 13:11). As for himself, he acknowledged his sin: "How many are mine iniquities and sins? Make me to know my transgression and my sin" (Job 13:23).
>
> However, he also said, ". . . I know that I shall be justified" (Job 13:18). Therefore he prayed, ". . . let not thy dread make me afraid" (Job 13:21).[8]

Dismay

The Hebrew term *châthath*[9] describes a person who "breaks down [mentally] by confusion and fear." One who is dismayed is drained of confidence and boldness to the point where he or she actually faints.

Our English word *dismay* probably comes from the Latin term *exmagare,*[10] *ex* meaning "out of, from." *Magare* is a word stem of Germanic origin akin to the Old High German *magan,* "to be able." Thus, to dismay is "to take away or remove the strength or firmness of mind which constitutes courage."[11]

Daniel fasted for an extended period of time. He had eaten no fine foods nor had he combed his hair. On the 21st day he was a wild-looking prophet walking on the shores of the Tigris River. Suddenly he looked up and saw one whose face was as bright as a flash of lightning. The men who were with him did not see anything, but they were terrified by the power they felt and so ran to hide. All alone and dismayed, Daniel dropped to the ground—unconscious.

But then he felt a strong hand lift him to his hands and knees. A voice spoke: "Do not be afraid, O man highly esteemed . . . Peace! Be strong now; be strong" (Daniel 10:19, NIV).

God's people tend to be intimidated by the strength of evil. The AIDS epidemic. The threat of nuclear war. The dramatic increase of drug and alcohol addiction. The government-sanctioned murder of millions of unborn babies. Couple all this with the apparent anemic condition of the Church and the exposed hypocrisy of well-known preachers and it's easy to feel ashamed, overwhelmed or dismayed.

Take heart. God told Joshua in the face of his internal anxieties and external worries, "Be not afraid, neither be thou dismayed" (Joshua 1:9). This same promise transcends both time and space to provide a tailor-made provision for us in the 20th century.

Terror

Terror is the most drastic form of fear, stripping one of both physical and mental capabilities.

Châgâ[12] is a term from an unused primitive root in the original Hebrew language which literally means "to revolve in a circle." It is likened to the giddiness or dizziness that is experienced after whirling around a number of times. Vertigo, confusion and bewilderment are a few of the results.

Can you imagine how the apostle John felt when he saw Jesus in His glorified form? White hair. Eyes blazing with fire. Two-edged sword protruding from His mouth. Face as bright as the sun. Brilliant robe with glory gleaming from every angle. Voice like a roaring waterfall. John's response? Terror. Absolute terror.

During my high school years I enrolled in shop class. I became dangerous in everything from arc-welding and wood-working to black smithing and auto-mechanics. One of the bits of information that happened to lodge between my ears after all that training involved transformers: those marvelous devices that take electrical power from one circuit and deliver it at a different voltage to another. I was especially interested in step-up and step-down transformers. The step-up type increase the voltage many times and are used in long-distance power lines. Just outside the limits of a small town, however, a step-down transformer is required so that the tremendous surge of voltage can be reduced. Otherwise every electrical appliance in that village would be blasted to smithereens.

God must use some type of step-down transformer in His relations with us humans. As created beings we can only handle a "few volts" of God at a time.

How does terror relate to the fear of the Lord? If we were able to see God's judgment upon sin, it would strike

terror in our hearts at the prospect of our personal engage-
ment in sin. There's no question about the fact that God is
serious. He is not to be trifled with. And those who mock
His principles will experience the terror of His judgment.
It is a motivation both for moral purity and for evangelism.

The apostle Paul was succinct in his explanation of
the happenings at the judgment seat of Christ. He stated
that no one would escape that appearance. He then followed it up with "knowing therefore the terror of the Lord,
we persuade men . . ." (2 Corinthians 5:11).

Balancing Fear

The fear of the Lord may have a paralyzing effect
on you. You feel like one wrong move and you're history.
The magnitude of God's awesome character *can* be overwhelming. But before you give up hope, consider this selec-
tion from *The Overlooked Requirements for Riches, Honor
and Life:*

> When God tells us to fear Him, He is requiring us
> to acknowledge an aspect of His character such as His
> justice, His holiness or His power.
>
> For each one of these attributes, God has a balanc-
> ing attribute. For His justice, He shows mercy. For His
> holiness, He gives grace. For His power, He displays
> lovingkindness. The more we understand, acknowledge
> and fear the first set of attributes, the more faith, hope
> and confidence we have in the balancing set of qualities.
>
> A person with little faith but a great awareness of
> God's power, justice and holiness will be out of balance
> in his fear of the Lord.
>
> In order to have a proper fear of the Lord, a person
> must increase his faith in the attributes which balance
> the ones that he fears. This balance of fear and faith is
> illustrated throughout Scripture.[13]

Fear Brings Integrity

There's an enemy to the fear of the Lord. It is known by several names: Indifference. Casualness. Apathy.

The manager of a large hotel in a world-famous American city related a stunning story a few years ago. His hotel hosted a conference for Christian youth workers and leaders, and during that particular weekend the X-rated in-room movie channels had a sudden, unusual surge in viewership. Need more be said?

How we need the fear of the Lord in our hearts! Our standards for morality, righteousness and success change when we enter into His presence and begin to see Him as He really is. It is then, and only then, that we can see ourselves as we really are and our place in the whole scheme of things.

In his classic book *The Holiness of God,* R. D. Sproul dramatically describes the awesome spectacle of the prophet Isaiah's encounter with the King of kings during a routine visit to the temple. We join Sproul's narrative just after Isaiah has pronounced the utter anathema of God's judgment upon his head.

> Immediately following the curse of doom Isaiah cried, "I am ruined." I prefer the older translation which read, "For I am undone." We can readily see why more modern translations have made the change from *undone* to ruined. Nobody speaks today about being undone. But the word is more vivid in what it conveys than the word *ruined*.
>
> To be undone means to come apart at the seams, to be unravelled. What Isaiah was expressing is what modern psychologists describe as the experience of personal disintegration. To disintegrate means exactly what the word suggests, *dis integrate*. To integrate something is to put pieces together in a unified whole. When schools are integrated, children from different races are placed

together to form one student body. The word *integrity* comes from this root, suggesting a person whose life is whole or wholesome. In modern slang we say, "He's got it all together."

If ever there was a man of integrity it was Isaiah Ben Amoz. He was a whole man, a together type of a fellow. He was considered by his contemporaries as the most righteous man in the nation. He was respected as a paragon of virtue. Then he caught one sudden glimpse of a Holy God. In that single moment all of his self-esteem was shattered. In a brief second he was exposed, made naked beneath the gaze of the absolute standard of holiness. As long as Isaiah could compare himself to other mortals, he was able to sustain a lofty opinion of his own character. The instant he measured himself by the ultimate standard, he was destroyed — morally and spiritually annihilated. He was undone. He came apart. His sense of integrity collapsed.[14]

The exciting conclusion to this event came when God asked, "Whom shall I send?" To which Isaiah replied in a quavering voice, "Here I am, send me." In so many words Jehovah said, "Aha, now we can get down to business. I can finally use you in a manner that will surpass your wildest dreams." Just think, God used a man who had just declared himself unclean! History bears out that God commissioned and used a regular rock of Jell-O. There's hope for you and me.

If our self-image, our conscience or our concept of integrity is based upon anything other than who God is, we're in for a rough time. On an individual basis we must continually be shaken to the very core of our hearts with the revelation that God is holy. He is not mocked. His standards are not to be trivialized. Before we can spiritually mature, we need to be stripped down by Him to see our total depravity.

But God...

Scripture tells us the bad news: We're corrupt, wicked and deceitful. We, however, are not left hanging in depression or hopelessness, because then comes the good news, the "But God's . . ." of the Bible.

BAD NEWS	GOOD NEWS
● In the past you were spiritually dead because of your disobedience and sin. At that time you followed the world's evil way; you obeyed the ruler of the spiritual powers in space, the spirit who now controls the people who disobey God. Actually all of us were like them and lived according to our natural desires, doing whatever suited the wishes of our own bodies and minds. In our natural condition we, like everyone else, were destined to suffer God's anger (Ephesians 2:1-3, TEV).	● *But God's* mercy is so abundant and his love for us is so great, that while we were spiritually dead in our disobedience he brought us to life with Christ. It is by God's grace that you have been saved (Ephesians 2:4,5, TEV).
● For no one is put right in God's sight by doing what the Law requires; what the Law does is to make man know that he has sinned (Romans 3:20, TEV).	● *But* now *God's* way of putting people right with himself has been revealed (Romans 3:21*a*, TEV).
● For sin pays its wage—death (Romans 6:23*a*, TEV).	● *But God's* free gift is eternal life in union with Christ Jesus our Lord (Romans 6:23*b*, TEV).

Left with only the bad news, we all would be forced to grapple with various options: 1. commit suicide; 2. form new philosophies (e.g., God does not exist; therefore who, cares? Eat, drink and be merry); 3. try gallantly to live according to God's laws without God's provision and power.

The "But God" factor strikes again! His good news gives us another choice: 4. receive His mercy and live for Him. Trials, tribulations and disillusionment will still confront us at every turn, "But God."

We could call it the "Ratchet Wrench Effect." A ratchet wrench must be turned backwards before the proper pressure can be applied to either tighten or loosen the bolt. What appears to be a move in the wrong direction, then, actually is a move forward when considering the entire process.

So it is in the way God deals with us. We must be impacted with the fear of God which causes us to be "undone" (a move seeming to be in the wrong direction) before we can fulfill the specific purpose to which each of us has been commissioned (a definite move in the right direction). This happens at each new level of growth.

Spiritual "Giants"

Recently I was ushered into the presence of God while reading Watchman Nee's book *Spiritual Knowledge.* He said that many are deceived when they evaluate themselves in their own dim light. They use an inferior standard and consider themselves to be quite holy and mature. Like Isaiah, though, the nearer we are to Him, the higher our standard of holiness and integrity become and the more we will discover what uncleanness, corruption and righteousness really are. It all centers around God and His glory.

Watchman Nee then went on to place some excellent and seasoned saints of God on open exhibit. I will borrow from his writings as we see how some of these great, spiritually advanced men of God viewed themselves in the light of God.[15]

Daniel. In the Bible there are only two major characters whose sins are not recorded. Daniel was one of them. The study of his life yields much insight into the fruits of a good conscience. Yet when in God's light he said, "There remained no strength in me; for my comeliness was turned into corruption, and I retained no strength. Yet I heard the voice of his words; then was I fallen into a deep sleep on my face, with my face toward the ground" (Daniel 10:8,9). When in God's presence, even this saint of saints could not stand up. He fell with his face to the ground.

Habakkuk. He was a mighty prophet of God who foresaw the captivity of Judah by the Babylonians. He asked God some burning questions about His justice and ultimately expressed confidence in His wisdom. But when in God's presence, he said, "I heard and my body trembled, my lips quivered at the voice; rottenness entered into my bones, and I trembled in my place" (Habakkuk 3:16).

Peter. He was the epitome of self-sufficiency. It was a different story, though, when he met the light of Jesus Christ—he couldn't help but confess his sinfulness. Remember the time when the disciples fished all night and caught absolutely nothing? Jesus ordered them to put their nets over the other side of the boat. Their catch was so huge that it took two boats to contain the multitude of fish. When all was said and done Peter fell at Jesus' feet saying, "Depart from me; for I am a sinful man, O Lord" (Luke 5:8).

Paul. He was a five-star general in the Lord's army. Paul was the man who said, "I am what I am by the grace of God" (1 Corinthians 15:10). As he grew closer to the Lord he said, "I am less than the least" (Ephesians 3:8). Prior to his grisly departure from this world (beheaded for the cause of Christ) he stated, "I am the chief of sinners" (1 Timothy 1:15). Paul was so aware of God's holiness that he considered himself to be worse than the rest.

The prolific writer Oswald Chambers commented

that once a person has seen himself in God's light he knows there is hope for all others. The person who has truthfully seen himself will never condemn another, nor will he spend an inordinate amount of time analyzing himself. The cross of Jesus Christ is that place of self-revelation.

The bottom line is that the sooner we realize that we are nothing but quivering blobs in comparison with God's glory, the sooner we can truly enjoy, with boldness, the exalted position that Jesus has given. Hang in there. In a future chapter we're going to discover some absolutely thrilling facts regarding our position and authority in Christ!

Bert and Ferd understand what it is all about.

Points to Ponder

1. Do you ever dwell on the "bad news" described in this chapter without following it up with the "good news"? If so, memorize at least one of the "But God's." Think of a way in which God's good news of mercy has set you free recently.

2. How would you react if Jesus, in His glorified form, appeared to you at this moment? How would your life be changed?

EIGHT

Confessions of An Approval Addict

*Seek popularity where it counts—
at the throne of God.*

I just finished doing it. It was a strange feeling—walking around the house with a pair of binoculars up to my eyes. Have you ever tried it?

Go ahead. Take a break. Grab a pair of binocs and bring your world into focused magnification. Cut out your peripheral vision by covering up the sides with the palms of your hands. Everything will look enormous. Start walking in a straight line toward a piece of furniture or a wall. You'll be tempted to probe ahead with a foot or hand. You'll experience a strong urge to peek periodically to establish your bearings. Resist all temptations!

Now, flip them around. Keep moving about. What a strange feeling! Everything appears to be so far away. Does *Gulliver's Travels* mean anything to you?

You have just encountered a profound concept. I call it the "Binocular Effect." (Creativity strikes again!)

Most of us spend a lot of time comparing ourselves

with the people around us. When doing so, one of two things occur. Either our heads swell up because everyone within our social environment seems to be so tiny. Or we suffer through a season of pinheadedness because everyone around us seems to be so huge. Herein lies the seduction that tries to ensnare Christians: letting go of Christ's standards and establishing a righteousness that is dependent on others' standards.

Recently, a pastor's wife said in exasperation, "I hate the virtuous woman in Proverbs 31. I can't identify with a perfect person who rises early, works industriously, enjoys a perfect family life, invests wisely, has time for the poor, has a word of wisdom for every situation, and works all night. She drives me batty. Compared to her, my life is an absolute mess."

Conversely, a young man carefully chose his words when talking about his wife, "I don't know quite how to put this, but my wife is totally different from me. Quite frankly, she's an airhead. She's scatterbrained. She's late for *everything*. She's forgetful. We're on totally different intellectual planes. We can't discuss anything intelligently. I'm not saying she's stupid or anything . . . well, maybe I am."

Sure, these are rather extreme examples, but they illustrate the two views that a pair of "binoculars" provide when we compare ourselves with the people around us. If we walk around life using a pair of binoculars, we're headed for trouble. Our view of ourselves becomes dependent on others, and soon our self-image is completely out of focus.

To some the fear of social rejection is a big issue, causing them to behave according to society's acceptance code. Others are obsessed with the fear of being taken advantage of. Many people are driven by the need for security. Others are plagued by the fear of sudden change while some become overwhelmed with fear of failure.

Approval Addiction Can Be Hazardous...

The inordinate need for approval is like an addiction. I know. I have been an approval addict for most of my life. *I've got to be positive, upbeat and happy. I can't let that glint of insecurity show in my eyes. Keep smiling. And don't let the nervous twitch in the right cheek show. No swallowing hard while talking — it's too obvious. I can't let anyone misunderstand my motives. Clarify and balance everything so that no one will get their feelings hurt.* One word of criticism from another person, one furrowed brow or one scowl used to send me into emotional shock.

In his book, *Feeling Good,* Dr. David Burns describes it well.

> Let's consider your belief that it would be terrible if someone disapproved of you. Why does disapproval pose such a threat? Perhaps your reasoning goes like this: "If one person disapproves of me, it means that everyone would disapprove of me. It would mean there was something wrong with me" . . . The price you pay for your addiction to praise will be an extreme vulnerability to the opinions of others. Like any addict, you will find you must continue to feed your habit with approval in order to avoid withdrawal pangs. The moment someone who is important to you expresses disapproval, you will crash painfully, just like the junkie who can no longer get his "stuff." Others will be able to use this vulnerability to manipulate you. You will have to give in to their demands more often than you want to because you fear they might reject or look down on you. You set yourself up for emotional blackmail.[1]

Obviously, approval feels good and we all need it at times. A word of encouragement and support can go a long way in improving our interpersonal relationships. In fact, we could use more positive reinforcement to ease the burdens that we all carry in this cruel world.

It is also a reality that rejection and disapproval usually result in uncomfortable, sometimes repulsive, feelings. This is easy to fathom. If we continue, however, to believe that approval and disapproval are the ultimate yardsticks with which to measure our worth, we are plunging ourselves into emotional quicksand.

Let's take a look at the price paid because of an unrestrained craving for social endorsement:

1. *Avoiding conflict at all cost.* Flight vs. fight. Tendency towards self-pity when one's spirit is wounded. It's easier to run from the pressure and bottle up the bitterness. It will explode on some later date at some seemingly insignificant event. Inner anger. Revengeful. Hard to forgive.

2. *Fishing for compliments.* Question to wife after Sunday sermon: "How do you feel the service was today?" Underlying questions—"How was my performance? Did the content and presentation of the message meet with everyone's approval?" Needing to know the latest public opinion poll of "yours truly" can result in a desperate existence.

3. *"I told you a million times never to exaggerate."* There were 100, maybe 125 people at the meeting. Actual count—97 people. *Maybe they will be impressed with me if I puff myself up and embellish my accomplishments just a tad.* Boasting—trying to cover up one's feelings of inferiority.

4. *"My favorite color is plaid."* Wishy-washy. Lack convictions—or at least the expression of those convictions when in the presence of people with strong personalities who possess conflicting ideas. Terrified by the mere thought of being rejected.

5. *Defense mechanisms.* Certain types of people and certain events produce automatic insecurity, fear and in-

timidation. Preach whole sermon at one person and afterwards he pumps my hand saying, "Great message! I hope *they* were listening." Ugh!

6. *"I'm stupid (but I hope you don't agree)."* Deep discouragement. Sigh. Look over at wife and say, "I'm no good. I might as well quit what I'm doing. I'm dumb. I'll never make it." Another sigh. Hope she doesn't agree with my assessment. Pressure and stress provide the opportunity for negative thinking. Too introspective. Impatient with personal performance.

7. *"I'm calling my travel agent to book a guilt trip."* Easily manipulated by a sense of guilt. Leans toward fears. Easily slips into self-condemnation. Anxious. Depression prone.

8. *The yo-yo syndrome: Up. Down. Up. Down.* Emotional well-being dependent upon current environment. *He frowned while I was talking. Maybe he doesn't like me.* Big mood swings. Self-pity.

9. *Blame game.* Shifting the spotlight to other people. Everything just happens to be somebody else's fault. Dwells on blemishes. Poor self-image. Nitpicker.

10. *"I'll tear myself down before you get a chance to criticize me."* False humility. Exposes weakness inappropriately. Emotional exhibitionism. Self-degradation. External person looks relaxed and easy going, but internally is experiencing intense frustration. Self-persecution.

Any of these sound familiar? It's easy to see how the conscience could wreak havoc with an approval addict. It is also easy to comprehend how one who struggles with an inordinate need for social approval would have a hard time with godly integrity.

Approval Addicts Through the Ages

But we're not alone in this. Peter, one of Jesus' disciples, grappled with similar issues. At one point the apostle Paul went nose to nose with Peter for succumbing to the pressure applied by the local Judaizers.

Remember, Peter was the one who had received the vision on the housetop confirming the reality that the food considered unclean under the Levitical law was now accepted. Ah yes, fried pork rinds and chicken wings, here we come.

In the times of the early church, the Judaizers were the ones who hated the new-fangled beliefs. They spent much energy lobbying and filibustering for the retention of the traditional doctrines and practices. When they got hold of Peter, he didn't stand a chance. He melted under the heat and forsook God's mandates in exchange for approval and acceptance from a few zealots who possessed strong personalities.

When Paul caught wind of Peter's wimp-like stance, he "withstood him to his face" (Galatians 2:11). Not my idea of a pleasant confrontation. Much later, Peter acknowledged Paul's wisdom and expressed warm regard for him (2 Peter 3:15).

Several thousand years earlier, Aaron suffered from similar ego demands. At the top of Mount Sinai, Moses was receiving the Ten Commandments. At the foot of the mountain, Aaron was modeling a style of leadership called *compromise*.

When about halfway down the mountain, Moses heard the party music below. Upon arrival at the camp he observed naked people dancing energetically around a golden calf. Enraged, Moses smashed the stone tablets on the ground. "Hey Aaron, what's going on around here? I'm gone for just a short while and all hell breaks loose."

Aaron immediately blamed the people. Typical. "Well, Moses, you were absent a little longer than originally planned, so the people gave their gold to me. I threw it all in the fire and all of a sudden this golden calf popped out. The people began to hail it as the god that brought them out of Egypt. I didn't have the heart to stop them. You understand, don't you, Moses?"

What a preposterous excuse! His insatiable need for acceptance caused him to listen to the fickle desires of the people, to disobey God and then to concoct a wild tale to justify his disobedience.

Both of these stories, though, have "happy" endings. The transformation of these biblical characters is compelling. Peter was ultimately crucified upside down for his faith in Jesus. He didn't believe he was worthy to die in the same position as his Master. Without flinching, he died a martyr's death. Hardly a predictable end for an approval addict.

At 123 years of age, Aaron finally died, leaving a rich legacy of faithful service as the high priest of Israel. His passing triggered a remarkable response from the people. The entire nation mourned for thirty days. Much later, Aaron had the distinction of being referred to as a type of Christ (Hebrews 5:4,5).

Kicking the Approval Habit

Stories like this give me hope that approval addiction can be beaten. I have experienced a measure of growth in my life in this area. It hasn't come easily or quickly, and I am still in process, needing His grace every step of the way.

I'd like to mention some of the things that have helped me confront the "please-don't-reject-me" root issues in my life. Your life may have included or may include different events and circumstances to achieve similar results:

1. *The Word of God* — The Scriptures keep narrowing me down to eternal reality. I take great comfort in knowing that "he who began a good work in [me] will carry it on to completion" (Philippians 1:6). When confronted with unfair circumstances that kick up some old insecurities, I am reminded that I can experience great peace and nothing will offend me because of my love for His Word (Psalm 119:165). Fear is removed when I remember that "if God is for [me], who can be against [me]?" (Romans 8:31)

It is hard to fully explain or comprehend, but the more I have meditated upon the Word, the more internal strength I have appropriated. My weaknesses have, in fact, become strong points because of His grace (2 Corinthians 12:9,10).

2. *Discipline of the Holy Spirit* — One example of this directly relates to my work with professional athletes. In the past, part of my need for approval was revealed by the way I would work a conversation around to the subject of sports so I could casually inform the other person I was chaplain of the Washington Bullets basketball team. Immediately I would feel important upon the perception of the listener's interest in me becoming more apparent.

Approximately seven years ago, the Holy Spirit instructed me to cease talking to others about that aspect of my life unless someone else raised the subject. This was a much needed training period where He was dealing with my ego and my motives for service.

For over two years I obeyed. One day I was witnessing to a man about Christ and during our conversation I sensed the freedom to use an illustration from my work with one of the Bullets players. Ever since that time I have had the liberty to raise the subject even though I do so with the constant awareness of His honor and glory. God has given me a unique opportunity and I plan to be a wise steward of it.

3. *Tough Times* — In thirteen years (at time of writing) of full-time ministry I have planted three growing churches. I'm still a young man, but without a doubt, certain crises in the ministry have driven me to my knees. I have often said that for every second of public applause there have been hours of behind-the-scenes tears.

I'll never forget the time I had to dismiss the administrator of our church school. Swift action and firm leadership were required after verifying the sordid details of his sexual misconduct with one of the male students. Within 33 hours, 120 parents were assembled in front of me, and I was terrified. The school ultimately had to close. Situations like this helped smoke out my addiction to approval.

4. *Marriage* — It has been said that there is no relationship in the universe that exposes selfishness quite like marriage. In any other relationship (co-workers or friends, for example) we have the luxury of being able to walk away at a certain point. But in marriage there is a conscious decision to stay together for better, for worse, for richer, for poorer, in sickness, in health — till death do us part.

Laurie and I have long since made the commitment to recognize and acknowledge when we start using juvenile tactics in our relationship: silent treatment; blaming; shaming; shifting the focus back on the other's blemishes when personal root problems are being exposed.

More times than not, we have discovered therapeutic value in giggling about our childish attempts to cover up some weakness. Believe me — God has creatively used my marriage to help me confront my inordinate need for approval! (I think my wife is surviving the ordeal too.)

5. *Graduate School* — The first two semesters at Loyola College in Baltimore included theoretical studies, child development, psychopathology, family therapy, psychological testing. It was quite a fascinating mixture.

The clinical part of the program began in the third semester. The small-group meetings, interdisciplinary groups and one-on-one supervision by a professor all worked together, helping me confront my excessive need for approval. I had to learn how to critique others when they made case presentations to the group. The most challenging, though, was learning how to receive constructive criticism from the rest of the group whenever it was my turn to present a taped recording of an actual counseling session. By the end of the three year program, I was experiencing relatively few "butterflies" in my stomach before, during or after my turn to present. I was stretched both personally and professionally during my Pastoral Counseling studies.

6. *Writing* — I respect authors and editors; the process involved in writing and rewriting is fraught with assaults on the ego. Most authors view their manuscripts as almost-human entities: "Don't touch my baby."

In 1979 I wrote a thirty-five-page manuscript about missions work. It was sent to an editor and when I received it again, the number of cruel, red marks on the pages was almost too much to bear. Tears welled up in my eyes. *This manuscript no longer sounds like me. The "Freeman touch"* (whatever that is) *has been lost.*

My last book, *"God Is Not Fair,"* was rewritten five times in two years. By the third rewrite I was ready to trash the whole idea. I have settled down a whole lot since that time, though, and have learned to appreciate and respect the insights and abilities of editors. (This should win some brownie points from my editor. Maybe he'll let some things slide!) [*No way. Ed.*]

7. *Child-rearing* — It has been said that preacher's kids are usually the worst hellions. I wonder why? Maybe it is because they've been told to shape up because daddy is the pastor. "Don't embarrass our family name. Your behavior reflects upon our position in the church and the community."

On several occasions I have actually caught myself just before making similar remarks to our older son, David. Sure, he needs to understand the value of integrity and how it can have a godly effect upon those in the community, but when we place a good reputation on a pedestal as an idol to be worshiped, we are asking for trouble.

The less compliant a child is temperamentally, the more he or she will set out to destroy the family's name by rebellious behavior if the parents' need for approval is the primary motivation for discipline.

As I raise my children, I discover that I'm learning and growing too. Our children and the myriad of challenges associated with their raising have caused me to evaluate my motives on a number of occasions.

These are some of the things that have caused me to journey in search of that sometimes elusive state called maturity. The only type of growth I'm interested in, of course, is that which is centered around the person and work of Jesus Christ. That's the only standard for integrity.

Bert and Ferd haven't given up on me yet.

Points to Ponder

1. Do you ride the emotional roller coaster of an approval

addict? What has God used to bring a measure of stability in your life over the past few years? Celebrate the growth, even if it seems like insignificant progress.

2. How do you handle another person when you sense his (or her) inordinate need for approval? Do you confront it bluntly, ignore it or try to creatively help him to see the problem?

NINE

Jackass Theology

*Character is who you are
when nobody else is around.*
—*D. L. Moody*

Sir, could I buy your pants? They look like they would fit me. You see, I was on my way to a very important meeting and I just ripped my pants. Please help me. Let me have your pants," he pleaded. "Here's twenty dollars."

The polyestered, semi-businessman-type stood still for a moment, staring at the stranger from head to toe with a mixture of astonishment and cynicism. "N-no," he stammered. "I can't do that."

The video stopped suddenly at that point as the energetic host of the now defunct television game show *Anything For Money* turned to the contestants saying, "Well, what do you think? Did he keep his pants on or did he take them off and sell them to our man on the street? Make your decision as we go to a commercial message." Winking at those of us in TV-land, he pointed in mock-seriousness, saying, "Don't touch that dial!"

I was hooked. I endured the bombardment of Madison Avenue propaganda, waiting to see what the man on the street would do. One thing was for sure. If I were in

101

his situation, I wouldn't sell my pants for any price. Well, *almost* any price.

The television audience clapped and cheered on cue as the show returned following the break. After a brief introduction, the same video segment was played from the beginning again and came to the point where the man refused the offer. I chuckled nervously as I vicariously entered into the awkwardness of the situation.

"Thirty dollars. Or, how about fifty dollars? This is an emergency. I really need your pants," the game show's man said while flashing more bills.

"That's for my pants?" The victim seemed a wee bit more interested with the green stuff in plain view.

"Yes sir. But I need them now," he dead-panned.

"Right here?" He looked around at the people passing by on the busy sidewalk, unaware that a hidden camera was recording his look of utter embarrassment. "I can't do that!" he added emphatically.

The actor/"businessman" brushed aside the man's objections. "Okay then, how about seventy dollars? I really need your pants."

"Seventy dollars?" I could almost see the smoke rising as he mentally calculated the number of trousers he could buy for that amount.

"Will you do it?" the actor queried, glancing dramatically at his watch. "I'm almost late." He flashed some more cash. "Here's my final offer. One hundred and twenty dollars. Here, it's yours. Take it. Take it," he insisted. "I really need your pants."

I couldn't believe it! Right there, in broad daylight in the middle of a sidewalk near an active intersection, the man went for his belt. In a twinkling of an eye his pants hit the pavement.

Unbelievable! Anything for money! The TV show was appropriately named because the concept behind it keys in on a widely-held notion — *everybody has a price.*

What's Your Price?

In an issue of *Last Days Newsletter,* the late Keith Green's challenging message strikes home:

> A poll was taken in the U.S., and they asked men and women how much money it would take for them to agree to sleep with a stranger. The average amount for the men was $10. The average amount for the women was $10,000. But as the dollar amount got higher, almost everybody said, "Yes, I'd sleep with a stranger for a million dollars." And what I'd say to all of them is, "You're willing to be a prostitute. All you're changing is the price. You're willing to set aside your convictions for money. If you can be bought at any price, then God doesn't care about the price. He only cares that you can be bought."
>
> What's your price? At what point are you willing to disobey God? What is there that can buy you? Are you for sale? Is God for sale in your life? Is obedience for sale?[1]

The person who holds out for a million dollars may *feel* more righteous than someone who caves in at $100 or even $1,000, but we should be careful of congratulating ourselves for having "higher standards" than so-and-so. From God's point of view, *all* are foul sinners and therefore *all* are in dire need of His abundant mercy.

The first step to experiencing a life that pleases God is to admit that without God we all have a price. That may be a rude awakening to those of us who have hidden our carnality under the thin veneer of culture and religion. Regardless of the bent of our lower natures, whether we lean toward religiosity or lasciviousness, God has concluded that we *all* are prime candidates for His grace.

The Old Testament character Balaam had an "I've-got-a-price-but-that's-okay" gleam in his eye. Many Bible personalities committed evil deeds, yet none were more severely excoriated than the prophet Balaam.

Leaders in the early church warned their flocks against false teachers by likening those teachers to Balaam. Fasten your seatbelts. Peter, Jude and John said it like this:

> They have left the straight way and wandered off to follow the way of Balaam son of Beor, who loved the wages of wickedness. But he was rebuked for his wrong doing by a donkey — a beast without speech — who spoke with a man's voice and restrained the prophet's madness (2 Peter 2:15,16).

> Woe to them! They have taken the way of Cain; they have rushed for profit into Balaam's error; they have been destroyed in Korah's rebellion (Jude 11).

> Nevertheless, I have a few things against you: You have people there who hold to the teaching of Balaam who taught Balak to entice the Israelites to sin by eating food sacrificed to idols and by committing sexual immorality (Revelation 2:14).

What a final portrait! A false prophet. Stubborn. Rebellious. Greedy. Deceitful. Lustful. Heretical. Immoral. Yet at the same time the scriptural account from Numbers 22 to Balaam's death in Numbers 31:8 reveals that he was the spokesman of God on such matters as Israel's blessings and the coming of the Messiah. What an end for a man "who hears the words of God, who has knowledge from the Most High, who sees a vision from the Almighty" (Numbers 24:16)!

What epitaph would you like at your gravesite? If there were such a landmark, Balaam's tombstone would probably have this chiselled inscription:

> Here lies the infamous, self-willed prophet, Balaam, the son of Beor. He misused his gifts and his relationship with God for personal gain. Study his life and beware.

The same propensity to sin lies within you.

A Donkey's Tale

Let's pause here and see if we can glean some priceless principles from a tale of Balaam's ever-so-famous talking donkey. The year is 1449 B.C. We've happened upon the city of Heshbon, a fairly large community in northern Moab, situated about twenty miles east of the Jordan River. It's morning, and we see a villager standing in the road in front of his house . . .

Yossell, one of the city's up-and-coming bakers, groaned involuntarily as he reached down, picking the scroll off the dusty ground. "Drat, those parchment boys are always missing my porch," he muttered to himself while maneuvering his paunchy frame over the rough path back to his modest hut. Pini, his wife of twenty-nine years, was in the kitchen busily stirring a gurgling substance in the kettle over the open fire.

Yossell unravelled that day's edition of the *Heshbon Scrollette*. He scanned the top of the paper. ISRAEL DEFEATED AT AI, 36 DEAD, the headlines screamed. "Oy Vey!" Yossell exclaimed, "What's happening, now? The world is falling apart."

He turned the scroll to the classified section. In his heart of hearts was a burning issue—he needed a beast of burden to help with the bread-delivery expansion he was considering.

Aha, this was his lucky day! There was to be an animal auction that afternoon in the main square. Jackasses were to be featured first. Immediately, his mind began churning. *So much to do. Pini must mind the bakery shop. The silver coins are under the loose block in the wall. The animals must be tested before the auction starts.* He whirled into action, giving detailed instructions to a less-than-delighted wife, rushing through chores, jogging down the road leading to town.

Before he knew it, he was at the auction site, bidding eagerly on the beast that was his first choice. He loved it! The pungent odors. The raucous noise and disorder. The psychology of bidding. The entire scene was so different from the normal, hum-drum routine of his life. The price of the donkey that he had set his heart on went far beyond his budget. Half-heartedly he began bidding on a few others. They, too, were out of reach.

Finally, he casually raised his hand to buy a coarse-haired donkey with a classic case of middle-age-spread, expecting a few others to join in. No such luck.

"Going once. Going twice. Going three times. Sold!" the auctioneer squawked "Number 37. He's all yours!"

What an anti-climax! *Ten silver coins for this mangy critter,* he thought while trudging home with his new acquisition in tow. *What's Pini going to think?*

Upon his arrival at home, he tied the beast securely to a poor-excuse-for-a-tree in the back yard. He took a few steps backwards, put his hands on the bulging part of his anatomy where hips were supposed to be, and gazed at the donkey in a calculating manner.

"I guess you'll do," he ventured. "Scrub Brush! That's what I'm going to call you. Yeah, that's it. Scrub."

The freshly dubbed donkey lifted his head in an almost-human acknowledgment of his new name. Yossell could've sworn that he winked at him. And what about that curious twinkle in his eyes? For one brief, mysterious moment Yossell was mesmerized.

"What do you have here?" His wife's shrill voice jerked him back to reality. "It's ugly! Couldn't you do any better than that flea-bitten thing?"

He snapped out of his contemplative pose, turning swiftly, muttering under his breath while sweeping past his wife and into their habitation.

The next morning Yossell's internal alarm buzzed precisely at 3:45. Pini stirred as he gently rolled out of bed. He froze until her breathing returned to normal rhythm.

He donned the worn-but-familiar tunic, splashed some water on his face and raced out and around the corner to fire up the bakery ovens.

The morning passed quickly. Early afternoon found Yossell excitedly loading Scrub Brush with bread to embark upon his entrepreneurial enterprise. The donkey swayed awkwardly under the weight as they headed down the road to set up shop in the main square.

Sweet success! Within an hour, Yossell had sold all of the loaves with orders for more in the future. Visions of grandeur danced in his mind as they trekked back home.

"Well, we sold all the bread!" he uttered in an exuberant, uninhibited manner. He slapped his beast good-naturedly on the rump, causing an eruption of restless flies amid a cloud of dust. "What do you think, Scrub?"

"Heh, I'm excited!" he responded.

Yossell proceeded a few more steps, took a double take and then stopped short on the lonely path. He paused and shook his head. "Naw, it couldn't be," he whispered. "I must be working too hard. That donkey didn't talk."

By now Scrub Brush was motionless, head turned in his direction.

"No, you heard correctly. I can talk." Then he laughed, releasing a long, harsh-sounding bray.

Yossell stared blankly, mouth ajar. He was speechless.

"I'm going to let you in on a secret. See that rock over there? Go on over and sit down. I'm going to tell you something that few others know."

Yossell was still in shock as he obediently shuffled over to the appointed spot and sat.

"I could tell by the response today that you are going to be extremely prosperous in the bakery business. Because of that, you will probably be confronted with issues you never before have had to face. Your major challenge will be to maintain a grip on right priorities and values."

By now Yossell had recovered sufficiently to frame a fundamental question. "How can you talk? You're an animal."

"Yes I am," he agreed. "Have you ever heard of the prophet Balaam?"

"Yeah, wasn't he the guy who King Balak hired to curse Israel a few years ago? There were a lot of jokes floating around about him. He certainly was a phony!"

Scrub Brush nodded. "You're right. I ought to know. He was my master."

"He was your master?" Yossell queried incredulously. He had his head in his hands. "I can't believe it. I can't believe it. Here I am, sitting on a rock, talking with a donkey I bought at an auction that claims he used to belong to Balaam. I must be hallucinating."

"No you're not," Scrub responded. "We have some time. Let me give you the inside scoop on what caused Balaam to be deceived."

"Go right ahead," Yossell ventured.

"Balaam bought me about ten years ago. At that time, he was a tender-hearted man — always helping people, cheerful. He had an intense desire to honor Jehovah in everything he did and said. I used to marvel at the way he consistently expressed his dedication and faithfulness to God. Everyone loved him. He had a great reputation. I was proud to be his donkey.

"But then something happened. To this day, I don't know what brought it on, but all of a sudden he developed a negative attitude. Even though he *never* let it show to anyone else, I saw it. When we were traveling alone he would mutter under his breath about the unfairness of life and use foul language at the slightest provocation.

"Over the months, he became cold, calculating and bitter. I could sense that he was increasingly competitive and jealous when in the presence of other prophets of God. I was dismayed. I thought that all the prophets were on the same team. He became the master of one-upmanship.

"Balaam began to compare the humble lifestyle of an itinerant prophet with that of established people who were wealthy and rich. He used to grumble and complain about that a lot. He'd say, 'I deserve more out of life.'

"Through it all, Balaam's miracle and teaching ministry was unbelievable! People were actually being helped. I couldn't understand how he could be so blessed—a man with a disintegrating behind-the-scenes character displaying a public ministry that seemed to have the anointing of God upon it. I was confused."

Yossell sat listening intently, chewing on a blade of grass. Scrub Brush paused, putting his head down to nibble on a clump of vegetation.

"I've heard a bunch of stories about Balaam. Did he ever regain his tender heart toward God?" asked Yossell.

"It is interesting that you should ask that question," the donkey responded. He finished chewing and gulped down what remained.

"I remember one time when he was sick with fever.

During this period I heard him praying and singing. It was a unique experience. His whole life took on a new sweetness for a few weeks. I never heard all the particulars, but it was as though he had experienced a spiritual renewal in his relationship with the Lord. But then his attitude changed again and he began to be mean and more blatant about his feelings regarding the unfairness of life."

"Balak, the former king of Moab, must've been desperate in order for him to pick such a loser like Balaam," Yossell proclaimed with a slight laugh.

"Well, you've got to remember," the jackass countered, "Balak had heard the chilling news about Israel's annihilation of the Amorites and he had done some hard-core analysis of the situation. No current military strategy would have been able to defeat Israel's God, and Israel's tents were pitched in the plains of Moab. They were prepared to attack at any time.

"Meanwhile, Balaam's reputation as a curse-'em-and-they'll-be-cursed, bless-'em-and-they'll-be-blessed type of guy had spread throughout the land. After all, who would hire somebody to come and curse his enemies if he didn't think it was going to work? So Balak sent some of his princes loaded down with money to recruit Balaam to curse Israel.

"I remember the glint in Balaam's eyes when he saw the gold that was being offered to him. I could almost read his thoughts: *This is the chance I've been waiting for. Finally, I'm getting compensated handsomely for all my hard work.* But he kept his emotions in check.

"I then remember the pious sound of his voice when he asked Balak's representatives to spend the night while he consulted God to see if he could go with them. I could read him like a book. What a phony! Balaam's eyes were blinded by the lust for position and wealth.

"About 2 o'clock in the morning, he came busting out of the house, untied me and jumped on my back. We then rode at a furious pace till we were outside the town limits. He then let out a long string of expletives at God. It was scary seeing a mere mortal silhouetted against the moon with upraised fist. It was obvious to me that Jehovah God had told him *not* to go."

"What did Balaam do then?" Yossell asked with growing interest.

"Balaam sent the first delegation away only to have a larger bunch of even higher-ranking officials return, upping the ante. Boy, did that ever stroke his ego.

"But you should've seen him. He was a confused mess. On the one hand God had clearly told him not to go, while on the other hand, his rebellious heart was seeking for a way to receive the wealth and status that would come with accepting the assignment.

"The next morning," Scrub continued after a slight pause, "He saddled me and we followed in the dust of Balak's ambassadors. About an hour after we left the house, the trail led us through a narrow, rocky gorge. We were plodding in single file. All of a sudden I looked up and saw an angel with a drawn sword. The immediate emotion I experienced was fear. Total fear! That angel was serious!

"Obviously, Balaam didn't see the angel, because when I balked he began to beat me furiously. Finally, I crushed his foot real hard against a huge boulder. He bellowed some choice words and the princes stopped, craning their necks to see why this hot-shot prophet of God couldn't handle his donkey. They obviously couldn't see the angel either."

"What happened then?" Yossell asked, breathless.

"Well, I hollered back. I said, 'Hey, what have I ever done to you to deserve these beatings?'

"To which Balaam retorted, 'Because you've made a mockery of me.' He was so humiliated and embarrassed! His fury then rose to the boiling point and he shouted, 'If there had been a sword in my hand, I would have killed you by now.' Can you imagine the scene?

"The angel then spoke. Balaam was told that if I hadn't stopped, his head would have rolled upon the ground.

"I couldn't comprehend the sheer audacity and wickedness in Balaam's answer to the angel. He responded with feigned repentance. He said, 'I have sinned. I didn't realize that you were standing in the way. *If* you are displeased, I will go back.'

"*If! If! If!*" Scrub emphasized. "Can you believe that he started the sentence with *if*? Here Balaam's life is hanging by a thread and he dares to say with baby-like innocence, 'If you are displeased . . .'

"I was trembling. At that point, I knew there was no turning back. Balaam had chosen the rebel's path. He wouldn't go back in repentance and he couldn't curse Israel. God wouldn't let him.

"What followed was absurdity to the umpteenth degree. King Balak chose three progressively higher hills from which Balaam was to pronounce a curse upon Israel, but each time Balaam opened his mouth he would utter a glowing blessing upon the nation of Israel. You should have seen the disconcerting countenance upon Balaam's face and the look of growing anger upon King Balak's — such irony! I must confess that I did chuckle reverently a few times.

"Ultimately there was no gold for Balaam. No high status. No warm applause in the Moabite palace. And no approval from God. Such is the fool's lot in life," the donkey commented thoughtfully. "After this event I left Balaam's care late one night and lost track of him. I did hear, though, that his behind-the-scenes, anti-Israel counsel to Balak was carried out."

"And what was that?" Yossell asked, scratching his nose. "Wait a minute. It's getting late. Let's talk while we walk."

"Good idea," Scrub replied, turning toward the crude path. "Remember the plague a couple of years ago that wiped out 24,000 Israelites?"

"Yeah."

"Well, that plague was the result of Israelite men fornicating with Moabite women and joining in their pagan sacrifices to Baal. I remember Balaam's final words to Balak, 'I'm sorry. Jehovah isn't allowing me to curse Israel, but you really don't need me. Send your prostitutes and 'easy' women to their men. Instruct the women to invite them to your Baal worship services and you'll draw the heart of the entire nation away from the one who won't let me curse them. Let their sin curse them. Sin will take care of everything for you. Get the picture?' "

They walked for a short while in silence. Both were in deep thought. As they neared the outskirts of town, Scrub Brush stopped suddenly.

"Yossell, I have some final things to say. As I said before, your bakery business has the smell of success. I want to share some time-tested principles that will help you keep a grip on right priorities regardless of what happens in your life. I've seen many people start out right and then lose their perspective. Here are ten basic principles:

"1. Keep your heart tender toward God—*always*.

"2. Keep the eternal perspective in clear view.

"3. Keep your heart pure through daily meditation upon God's Word and prayer.

"4. Keep short accounts with God and the people in your sphere of influence.

"5. Love your wife.

"6. Be bold in your witness to others.

"7. Do the details with dignity. God is your audience.

"8. Give freely of your time, abilities and money. You can't outgive God.

"9. Never let bitterness fester in your heart.

"10. Never lose your sense of humor or zest for living."

"Whew, that's a mouthful. I feel overwhelmed," Yossell sighed.

"Don't worry," Scrub said, moving forward again, "You do the *following after God* and He will do the *transforming of you.*"

Pini almost flew out the front door as the pair approached. "How did you do? Anything exciting happen today?" she cried breathlessly.

Yossell hugged her. "Yes, my dear, this has been an unusual day. But then, you wouldn't believe it!" He peeked over his wife's shoulder, winking broadly at Scrub Brush.

Scrub returned the wink, saucily threw back his head and let out a characteristically raucous bray.

Bert and Ferd were there.

Points to Ponder

1. Tough question. At what price would you consider sleeping with a stranger? It would only take thirty minutes of your time in bed. And you could compose your prayer of repentance in advance. Be honest.

2. How does motivation affect ministering? How can you determine your motives?

3. What can you learn from Balaam's life? How will this touch your life tomorrow?

TEN

Pet Peeve #98

O Lord, open blinded eyes and
bring renewal, beginning with me.

Pet Peeve #98: Out-of-focus slide shows. Don't you hate them? You know what I mean.

Close friends return from a vacation where they spent their leisure time on an exotic, little-known Caribbean island. Herb took tons of pictures while he and Gertrude were away. The first thing he did when they returned home was to get the slides developed. A few days later you were invited for dinner to share in their memorable experience.

Ooh, the dinner was excellent! You burp quietly. Satisfied, your stomach growls passively. The internal beast has been tamed for another few hours.

"Come down to the basement," Herb purrs excitedly. "I've got the slide projector and screen set up. I can't wait till you see the pictures. They're bee-yoo-tee-ful!"

You extricate yourself from the chair somehow and waddle dutifully behind him. The window shades are already drawn on the lower level of their home. The over-stuffed chairs are in place with everyone having front row seats. Four *National Geographic* magazines are stacked neatly under the front end of the slide projector, providing a precise 23° angle shot at the screen.

Herb clicks the projector on. Gertrude stands by the light switch and turns the overheard lights off on cue. The first slide image appears on the screen. Herb manually turns the lens back and forth until the picture is focused to his satisfaction. You strain your eyes at the still ever-so-slightly-blurred beach scene.

You look over at Herb. His beatific smile is outdone only by the reflective gleam bouncing off his glasses. He seems to be oblivious to the fact that the image on the screen is still fuzzy. You clear your throat noisily, "Herb, don't you think that the picture could use a little focusing?" You try to be as tactful as possible.

Herb is an accommodating sort of chap, so he gallantly tries to bring it into focus. "How's that?" he queries.

"Well, it could be better."

He tries again. "Is that better?"

"Yup." You've known Herb for years, but this is the first time you've discovered that, plain and simple, he just doesn't have a good eye for focus. You can quickly see that every new slide is going to rile up your Pet Peeve #98. So, you settle down for the next hour allowing the narrators to fill in what your eyes miss.

Would you believe it if I told you that God invented Pet Peeve #98? Think about it. Try to imagine how God must feel when we allow the sands of time to distort our vision of the value of the eternal.

God loves to have pure, unadulterated fellowship with us on a continual basis. He must grieve when we allow materialism, spiritual apathy and other forms of disguised pride to get our lives out of focus.

When we choose to function in this manner, God, motivated by perfect jealousy, allows certain crises to develop within our lives. Are the trials caused by Satan or by God? Are they the consequence of a series of bad decisions? Are they the culmination of a myriad of natural causes? There are no easy answers. The focal point, though, is that the emotional pain caused by hard times causes us to reevaluate our relationship with Him and motivates us to sharpen our concentration upon what will last forever.

Getting Out of Focus

Couples get married, have a baby and start missing Sunday morning services. Teenagers reach a certain age and say, "I'm not going to church anymore!" A businessperson becomes consumed by a seventy-hour-a-week schedule on his or her way to the top. It all starts so insidiously. The change is almost imperceptible. The private devotional time and passionate prayer begins to fall off. The conscience becomes darkened—little by little. Before you know it, spiritual matters are of little importance.

Many times it takes a crisis to grab our attention and to cause us to focus more crisply and clearly upon the King of kings and Lord of lords.

Take King David, for instance. In *The Myth of the Greener Grass,* J. Allan Petersen says it well:

David was just coming off a season of prosperity and fame.

In numerous battles he had been victorious; he had destroyed 87,000, captured 22,000. And all these victories were confirmations of God's presence within him and of God's promise to give him an eternal dynasty. "So the Lord gave him victories wherever he turned."

God's promises had just been uttered: "I chose you; I have been with you. You will become one of my most famous men in the world. Your family shall rule my kingdom forever." And David responded with over-whelming thanks: "Why have you showered your bless-ings on me? Such generosity is far beyond any human standard. You have done great miracles: may you be eter-nally honored. You are indeed God, your words are true."

He had just previously gone out of his way to keep his vow to Jonathan and had restored to his heirs all the land formerly owned by Saul. Jonathan's lame son was invited to live at the palace as one of David's own fami-ly. Unashamedly, David had danced before the Ark of the Lord in the sight of the whole city in celebration, in praise of God. "I am willing to act like a fool in order to show my joy in the Lord," he said . . . So here's David, a man of great courage, generosity, and kindness, just and fair in his dealings, committed to God and full of praise and thanksgiving.[1]

Yet, in the lining of this fluffy cloud of prosperity was an ominous, foreboding thunderbolt. God allows us to see David's flagrant display of human nature—warts and all. Adultery with Bathsheba. The murder of Uriah. Con-sistent weakness in disciplining his sons. The list goes on. His view of eternal values ran the gamut between crisp and blurry. There were a number of occasions when God per-mitted tough times in David's life to help him refocus.

David's Crises

Let's define the word *crisis*. A crisis is any ex-perience that challenges your structured mentality and forces you to change—whether it is a "happy crisis" (mar-riage, birth of child or job promotion) or the emotional trauma resulting from tragedy (car accident, cancer or a friend's death).

What, then, was the most change-producing experience in David's life?

Was it when, as a young shepherd, he had to kill a ferocious bear or a raging lion? I'm sure that either occasion caused his adrenalin to pump wildly.

Was it when he was standing in the shadow of the great prophet, under the jealous gaze of his brothers, feeling the oil oozing over his curly, red hair and hearing Samuel say, "I now anoint you to be the next king over Israel"? Try to imagine the content of the thoughts that must have been racing through his mind. What a shock — from the pasture to the palace!

Was it when he was softly plucking his harp in the torch-lit chambers of the king, and Saul grabbed his javelin, lurched forward and hurled his weapon straight at David? After which David cried (in the original Hebrew language), "Feet don't fail me now!"

Was it when he ran toward the 9 foot, 6 inch Goliath, yelling, "You're dead meat!"? The eyes of all Israel were fastened upon this young man as he, with slingshot in hand, drew closer to the infamous, heavily armed foe.

Was it when he looked across the street while pacing restlessly across the walkway on the roof of his palace and saw the voluptuous form of Bathsheba? With hundreds of women at his beck and call, he certainly was no frustrated Peeping Tom searching for some voyeuristic thrill. Yet — was this the greatest crisis in his life?

Or was it a short while later when Nathan the prophet pointed a bony finger in David's face and said, "You are the man." From that point on David's whole kingdom took a downward turn.

Whew! It's no wonder the book of Psalms presents David as a towering, spiritual giant one moment and as a blubbering, neurotic wimp the next. His life seemed to be a roller coaster ride — high, mountain-top experiences followed by extreme valleys. He was the King of Crises. Always one hair's-breadth away from insanity.

Conscious of our own emotional hills and valleys, we relate well to the book of Psalms, because the writers so realistically picture our timeless search for fulfillment in life.

The psalms provide a gut-level, between-the-lines glimpse of what was really going on during actual events. For instance, Psalm 57 was written while David was hiding from Saul in the Cave of Adullam (1 Samuel 22:1). Psalm 56 was penned just after David feigned insanity and was subsequently released by his captors, the Philistines (1 Samuel 21:10-15).

Psalm 62 and 63 unveil David's emotional state during what Dr. J. Vernon McGee describes in *The "Only" Psalm*[2] as the greatest crisis that ever entered David's life. The event is chronicled in 2 Samuel 15. Follow the drama with me.

The Vision-Clearing Crisis

What a disheveled sight! A barefooted, sixty-five-year-old man picking his way along a rocky path. The soot from ashes smeared over his sweaty body. Pieces of sackcloth draped uncomfortably upon his head and frame. Tired lines creasing his countenance. Tears streaming down his face.

Atop the Mount of Olives, on the eastern side of Jerusalem, David paused reflectively, turning around to survey the pandemonium back at the city. Off in the distance, above the sobs and groans of the grieving loyalists milling about, he could hear the crowds shouting deliriously for his dearly beloved, but unfaithful, son: "Hail Absalom! Hail Absalom!"

He listened briefly to the fickle cry of the multitude

as Absalom entered triumphantly into Jerusalem. He knew the sting of the voices of the multitude and understood the dynamics of mob psychology. The same crowd that shouted, "David has killed his ten thousands!" was now yelling, "Absalom is our king!"

What a dramatic moment! What a time of decision! Some are choosing David; others are choosing Absalom. David is discovering the identities of those who blessed him with their mouths while cursing him inwardly.

Most notably, David's prime confidant and friend, Ahithophel (related by marriage through Bathsheba), felt the political winds change. He said, "My arthritis kicks up when I sleep in damp, dark caves. I'm too old for that sort of stuff anymore. Absalom is the new king. I have better social security benefits if I stay with him. So long, David."

The Judean wilderness looked barren and uninviting as the king descended from his vantage point. An urgent voice called his name. Blinking back the tears, he turned quickly to see Ziba, the servant of Mephibosheth (the crippled son of Jonathan). "Where is Mephibosheth?" he queried. There was cool aloofness in Ziba's tone as he responded, "Oh, he decided to remain in Jerusalem. He's deserted you in favor of Absalom."

David's heart dropped. *Oh no! It can't be! Not Mephibosheth! After all I've done for him? Wait a minute! Could Ziba be lying?*

He had no time to discern the truth of the matter. Too much was happening all at once. He quickened his step.

All of a sudden he felt pain at the right side of his head. Someone was throwing a volley of dirt and stones at him. A local rebel, Shimei, was crouched down about ten yards away with a devilish sneer upon his face. He scooped up a handful of pebbles for another attack. Instinctively, David's mighty men reached for their swords.

"You're a wicked, foul man of blood!" Shimei screamed. David ducked as he heaved another handful of rocks. "You deserve everything that's happening to you!" he snarled.

David's body stiffened. He hesitated for a second as he stared at this situational opportunist. The soldiers were poised, ready to separate Shimei's head from his shoulders at the slightest cue. The silence was deafening as every eye searched for clues on David's countenance.

"Don't touch him," David commanded. "Leave him alone."

A collective sigh of disbelief escaped. Yet, everyone turned in unison to continue the trek toward the Jordan River and beyond. Shimei followed — shrieking and cursing, while pelting the king from behind.

How strong were the seams of David's soul? What word would aptly describe the state of his emotions? Humiliation? Embarrassment? Bitterness? Shock? Denial? Rage?

Down to "Only"

Let's take a peek into David's inner world during this intense encounter with pain:

> Truly my soul waiteth upon God: from him cometh my salvation. He only is my rock and my salvation; he is my defense; I shall not be greatly moved (Psalm 62:1,2).

Can you see David's jaw jutted out in dogged determination? Can you picture his veins bulging in his neck? Do you see his eyes — looking straight ahead with a fixed purpose? While everything is crumbling around him, he's singing a "Hallelujah Chorus" on the inside!

I think it was Charles H. Spurgeon who was the first to call Psalm 62 "the *only* Psalm." Of course, there are 149 other psalms; it's just that in this psalm the little word *only* occurs four times.

Prior to this life-changing event, David had been sitting in the proverbial lap of luxury. He had enjoyed all the amenities that his position afforded—status, wealth and comfort. Anything his heart desired was his without question. But now he was narrowed down to "only."

I'll never forget the panic-stricken telephone call I received from a well-known former professional athlete. I'll call him Sam. He had achieved great heights of success and prosperity during his playing days. The statistics of his performance in his sport had dazzled the critics and fans alike during his career. But now something was different. There were no lights, no camera, no action. He was in the dumps.

I knew he was sitting behind his desk in the large overstuffed chair in his dark, shade-drawn office. Plaques, trophies and other memorabilia sagged lavishly over every possible open square inch on the walls.

"Pastor Freeman," he began, "I need help. I feel so depressed. I don't know what to do." He paused for a few moments. I heard his hand fumbling around with the mouthpiece of his phone. I could picture him trying to keep me from hearing his sobs and sniffles. My heart went out to him. I remained silent.

"I'm sorry," he continued, "this is the first time I've cried since I was a little boy."

After regaining his composure somewhat, he unravelled the details of his rocky marriage, the challenges from his rebellious children, the low morale of the people in his business, severe financial problems and difficulty in coping with life after professional sports. We talked for over an hour.

During the ensuing weeks and after a number of long-distance exchanges, Sam determined that God was narrowing him down to "only." All the other support systems that he had placed his trust in were now shifting and changing — hence a vision-clearing crisis.

Sam had a choice: Either he could continue with a defeatist mentality, resigning himself to giving in, or he could fight back in a positive manner by accepting the responsibility and challenge of facing his dismal circumstances with the power of faith in Jesus and His Word. He chose the latter.

Over the months, Sam has matured in the Lord. Not everything has turned out peachy-keen and he still struggles, but his ultimate focus is clear as he says with King David, "He *only* is my Rock and my Salvation!"

"I Shall Not Be Moved"

Like Sam, David adjusted to God's way of thinking. That's integrity. That's keeping the conscience pure. But there's something even more exciting:

> My soul, wait thou only upon God; for my expectation is from Him. He only is my rock and my salvation: He is my defense. I shall not be moved (Psalm 62:5,6).

Here we understand the deep, hidden secret to David's triumph over the enticing plunge into depression and discouragement. He reiterated and amplified his thoughts about the Lord, his strength.

I'd like to point out something. In verse two David says, "I shall *not* be *greatly* moved." In verse five, however, he says, "I shall *not* be moved. " Can you see it? As he continued to retain his clear view of God's sovereignty in spite of his circumstances, David's personal experience of God's promises became more cohesive and firm.

I can identify. I've been pastoring since 1975. I must admit, during the years there have been a number of times when I have come to the pulpit to preach feeling less than spiritual. If a loudspeaker had been affixed to the top of my

head during those moments, revealing my innermost
thoughts, the people probably would've heard some rather
uncomplimentary statements. As the pastor, though, I
could not be "greatly moved." It's not socially acceptable!
After reading the Word, however, and after ten minutes
into the message, each time I began to experience the
reality of what I was preaching. It wasn't long before I could
say with conviction, "I shall not be moved!"

"Trust in Him"

But David doesn't stop there. He goes on to say:

> Trust in him at all times; ye people, pour out your
> heart before him: God is a refuge for us. Selah (Psalm
> 62:8).

There's nothing inhibiting David's relationship
with God. No unconfessed sin—he's kept short accounts.
No guilt—whether pseudo or real. His conscience is clear.
No unhealthy fears—he recognizes that God is approachable. He now turns with authority to the people around him
who are following.

David has a unique boldness. He's not a modern person giving some vicarious thrill to a comfortable,
well-dressed audience. What he's saying has been written
in his own blood, sweat and tears. He's lost his throne. His
favorite son has betrayed him. The entire kingdom is in
upheaval. He's got my attention.

I have discovered most of the time we are able to
comfort others wherein we ourselves have been comforted.
When we have been through our own deep waters, God
grants us a greater capacity for understanding others.

Recently I sat across the dinner table from a pastor
who was smack-dab in the middle of an ugly church split.
He frequently wiped his tearstained eyes while describing
the juvenile behavior and fleshly tactics employed by most

of his congregation during this intense struggle for power.

When he finished I shared some thoughts with him about God's faithfulness and our responsibility to be faithful when others are unfair. I didn't necessarily think that what I said was exceptionally profound. Yet, he seemed to respond positively. Later, in fact, he wrote me a gracious letter, telling me how much my words had encouraged him. I was surprised by his unexpected expression of kindness and appreciation. I was just speaking out of my experience. If I had been a pastor who had run continually from pressure and played the blame-game, I would not have been able to testify of God's faithfulness.

If we "keep on keeping on," God shaves off some rough edges through various and sundry circumstances and then uses us to reach out and minister healing to those who are hurting.

"Power Belongs to God"

Is there more for us to see in David's soul during this traumatic event? Yes.

> God hath spoken once; twice have I heard this; that power belongeth unto God (Psalm 62:11).

With emphasis, David recognized that God held everything in the palm of His hand. Off in the distance, he could still hear the roar of the crowd proclaiming Absalom as their hero. Even though his temporal power-base was shifting, deep in his heart of hearts he knew God was in control. All power belongs to God. He exalts and He abases.

Recently, I watched with fascination a television special aired on the Public Broadcasting System about the advances and retreats of Hitler's forces in the Soviet Union during World War II. Against the counsel of his advisors, Adolf Hitler maniacally ordered the bulk of his vast army to march on Moscow. For months the world watched in horror as the troops from the Third Reich cut a swathe, at will, through the U.S.S.R., leaving ruin and destruction in their wake. Hitler appeared to be one giant step closer to fulfilling his dream of being the one to dominate the entire world.

As the Nazi troops approached, Moscow's citizenry hurriedly packed their belongings and vacated the capitol city — en masse. Flushed with the excitement of months of easy victories, the German soldiers converged upon the nearly empty shell of their primary target. Relatively few Soviet soldiers remained to resist the German army's advances; Hitler's conquest seemed imminent. For days, the skirmishes with Soviet troops held off the German occupation, but they couldn't hold out much longer.

But then it began to snow. And it snowed. And it snowed some more. The once-cocky German forces were ill-prepared for the rough Russian winters. The sub-zero temperatures dipped dangerously low. Their German tanks refused to start. Their German motorcycles and trucks were unwilling to turn over. Their German uniforms did not keep them warm. Morale was extremely poor.

The experienced Russian soldiers were emboldened by the apparent vulnerable condition of their adversary. Slowly but surely the Nazi's were driven into their only viable option — retreat. Some historians believe that this was the major turning point, helping to smash Hitler's diabolical plot for global triumph. It is my belief that God used the elements to quell Hitler's advances.

I find myself chuckling out loud as I reread the preceding historical account. And then I think of Psalm 2 where David talks about the rulers of the earth that gather together to take counsel against God. Here's God's response in verse 4: "He that sitteth in the heavens shall laugh: the Lord shall have them in derision."

God doesn't always choose to intervene in a

dramatic manner, but it is almost as if God sent the snow on Hitler's forces, laughing uproariously, saying, "Hey, Hitler! You think you're going to rule the world, eh? Well, you must reckon with Me first. Let's see if you can handle some cold weather." It was God's way of resisting the proud.

It's no wonder that at this crisis in his life, King David could cry out, "Power belongs to God!" He was not helpless against Absalom's tyranny. God and he were a majority!

"Mercy Belongs to God Also"

The final insight we can glean as we peek into David's inner world is found in the last verse of Psalm 62. Let's take a look at it:

> Also unto thee, O Lord, belongeth mercy: for thou renderest to every man according to his work (Psalm 62:12).

There it was, the ark of the covenant! Covered with the beautiful, ornately crafted mercy seat. The golden wings of the sculptured cherubim glinted in the late afternoon sun. Zadok, the high priest, ran toward David, his robes flapping and his hand waving. "O King, we got it out of the temple just in time!" he hollered while yet twenty yards away.

David waited for his breathless arrival. He appreciated Zadok's exuberance, but the decision was clear. The mercy seat must go back to the temple. Zadok and Abiather dutifully carried it back and remained in Jerusalem at David's request.

This, in my opinion, is the most touching aspect of the story. David's primary motivation in life was to give mercy as freely as he had received it. David left the precious mercy seat in Jerusalem, saying, "If God sees fit, He'll spare my life and I'll see it again."

The mercy seat was at the very core of the Jewish Old Testament religion. David was saying that God, who exercises all power, is also a God who administers His affairs with mercy. Mercy is at the heart of true authority.

David's focus upon mercy never ceases to amaze me. In fact, if we were to put this story on "fast-forward," we would encounter David's response to the news of Absalom's death.

In 2 Samuel 18 we pinpoint the events that led up to the fierce battle in the woods of Ephraim where over 20,000 men were killed. During that conflict, the captain of David's army, Joab, found Absalom dangling by his long hair from the stout bough of a huge oak tree. In an instant, Joab scored a bulls-eye as he hurled three darts into Absalom's chest. Absalom's body shook convulsively and then stilled. He was dead!

We're all happy, aren't we? No, not David. When a messenger broke the news to him, he wept, "O my son, Absalom, my son, my son Absalom! It would have been better that I had died in your place. O Absalom, my son, my son!"

Faith in God during trials and mercy to those who mistreat us. Obedience to God's ways is like a telescope that brings the eternal perspective into clear view. No more blurry slide shows for David.

Bert and Ferd are happy.

Points to Ponder

1. Have you become content with a blurry view of eternal values? If so, how can you sharpen your focus?

2. Read Psalm 62 and ask the Holy Spirit to reveal three principles that will benefit you.

ELEVEN

Live Right
Anyway!

*Some people like to live within the sound
of the church bell, but I'd rather run
a rescue shop within a yard of hell.*
—C. T. Studd

People are illogical, unreasonable, and self centered;
LOVE THEM ANYWAY!
If you do good, people will accuse you of selfish, ulterior motives;
DO GOOD ANYWAY!
If you are successful, you will have false friends and true enemies;
SUCCEED ANYWAY!
Honesty and frankness make you vulnerable;
BE HONEST AND FRANK ANYWAY!
The biggest people with the biggest ideas can be shot down by the smallest people with the smallest ideas;
THINK BIG ANYWAY!
People favor underdogs, but only follow top dogs;
FIGHT FOR AN UNDERDOG ANYWAY!
What takes years to build may be destroyed overnight;

BUILD WELL ANYWAY!

The good you do today may be forgotten tomorrow;

DO WHAT'S RIGHT ANYWAY!

People really need help but they attack you if you help
them;

HELP ANYWAY!

Sinners don't always want to hear the gospel;

WITNESS TACTFULLY ANYWAY!

Give the world the best you've got and you'll get
kicked in the teeth;

GIVE THE WORLD THE BEST YOU'VE GOT
ANYWAY!

Author Unknown

Grit your teeth. Make your eyes blaze with determination. Clench your fists. Take a deep breath and repeat after me: "Every time I am offered the choice between integrity and dishonor, I will honor God by choosing the way of integrity—no matter what it costs me."

I know. I know. Human willpower and strength by themselves don't amount to a pile of garbage in God's economy. But there is something to be said for stick-to-it-iveness. Old-fashioned faithfulness is refreshing, especially in an age of such rampant compromise.

Take Carole for instance. Both she and her husband George realized something was terribly wrong when her doctor bustled into the room. He had performed an amniocentesis a few weeks prior and had obtained the lab results. His furrowed brow and nervous manner spoke for themselves.

Carole, forty-three, a pretty brunette, was fourteen weeks pregnant. Her pregnancy had been a shocking surprise to both her and George. At first she had reacted negatively, but now she was actually looking forward to having a bouncing little baby around the house.

Instinctively, her emotions became numb. The doctor's words sounded hollow and hazy. "I don't quite know how to tell you this, but all the lab tests came back positive, with the clear indication that your child will probably have Downs Syndrome."

After explaining everything about the extra 21st chromosome, complete with a blur of incomprehensible medical terminology, and after enumerating the options that were available to them, he asked, "Do you want the responsibility of raising a mentally retarded child?"

There was a period of silence. It was obvious that, in the doctor's studied opinion, abortion was the more expedient choice. Carole and George looked at each other, each searching for clues on the other's face.

"Well, how long do we have before making a decision?" she finally responded.

"Hmm, let's see," he said reflectively, "a couple of weeks."

The next few days were tough for both of them. Even though they had been repulsed by the mere thought of abortion in the past, they had never expected to be confronted by the need to make a personal decision on the matter. It is impossible to recount the mood swings they experienced.

After reading literature on the subject and after much prayer and counseling they finally made a decision. They decided to keep the child.

This determination was based upon the conviction that life comes from God. Furthermore, human preference or convenience must never enter into the picture when considering the fate of someone else's life.

Their resolve to keep the child brought immediate peace. A little over five months later, Nathaniel George was born. The doctor's evaluation was correct. He was retarded.

Almost ten years have passed. Their entire lives have changed. They've been through some tough times, but they've never regretted the decision to keep "Great Nate," as he is called. Believe me, he's a wild character — full of fun and surprises.

God puts a high premium on faithfulness. I think that George and Carole are going to get tons of rewards when they get to heaven. They are my kind of heroes — people who dare to obey God regardless of the cost. They chose right anyway.

Arnie

Arnie is a streetwise twenty-year-old. He has grown up in a crime-ridden neighborhood with good-for-nothing friends, heavy metal music, occultic-styled tatoos, hard drugs and immorality galore. It hasn't been easy, being exposed to some of the harsh realities of life from an early age.

Yet, three years ago, he made his peace with God by accepting Christ as his personal Savior. Even though he continued living in the same environment, things have changed. No more glazed-over, hollow-looking eyes. No more wild late night parties. No more close brushes with the law.

What inspires me the most about Arnie is his enthusiastic consistency. Approximately twelve months ago, however, he was severely tempted to backslide. Some of his former girlfriends started coming around, flaunting their physical assets. He began bumping into his old partying buddies in the oddest places.

Meanwhile, the zest of his initial experience with the Lord seemed to be waning. His inner spiritual capacity felt dry. To top it all off, some "seasoned" Christians had treated him unfairly. The enticement of temptation plus his disillusionment with Christians was almost too much for him to bear.

I remember counseling with him during this testy period. We talked about eternal value. We discussed both the short-term and long-term benefits of obedience. After talking for a couple of hours, I finally said, "Arnie, I know you're being hit with every temptation and doubt imaginable, but please remain faithful to Jesus. He will reward you beyond your wildest dreams." He did some serious thinking.

And now, a year later, Arnie has been blessed with a new level of maturity. He has remained faithful and his heart is being established in grace. He lives right anyway.

"Mr. John"

I affectionately call him "Mr. John." He's a special man with a perpetually impish grin. He cooks for himself, dresses without aid and drives his own car. This is not exceptional until you understand that Mr. John is eighty-two years old and a paraplegic.

Twenty-two years ago, a church building literally caved in on him. Heroically, he threw his body across his granddaughters, sparing them from being crushed by the falling beams. This valiant act caused him to spend six months on a Stryker frame in an effort to straighten his body.

"It was terrible," John recounts. "I lived in constant pain and actually wanted to die. I had bad kidneys, crushed lungs, steady migraine headaches and bursitis. I refused to eat. Then a minister came in to talk with me. He encouraged me to accept what was happening and to go on."

John was in the hospital for two years before being able to return home. His wife died eight years later and the future looked impossible without her. But with prayer, God gave him the strength to accept her death and his disability. He, however, doesn't consider himself handicapped because he can do so many things "through God's grace."

Counting his many material blessings, John says, "I have a boat and a lift to get me in and out of the boat. It hooks to my wheelchair. I own a shore home on the Chesapeake bay and love to fish and crab. I realize that feeling sorry for myself will only make me more miserable. So, I do what I can to magnify Christ and enjoy life."

He has grappled with the seductive whisper of suicide. He has battled with the icy grip of self-pity. Doubts on every level have assailed him. He has been bombarded with every "why" question in the book. But you know what? He has won a tremendous victory. He has accepted God's sovereignty in the whole matter.

He makes a quiet impact upon everyone he meets. His life of integrity has touched me deeply. I thank God for Mr. John. His attitude is right anyway.

Harvey

He saw it coming. He veered his vehicle sharply to the left, hoping to miss the glaring headlights. It was a split-second decision. CRASH!

Harvey was a four-hour-old newlywed. He had just gotten married to a beautiful woman, Lucille, who was sitting beside him with wandering hands, periodically whispering "sweet nothings" in his ear. They were approximately thirty minutes away from their honeymoon bungalow in the mountains when a drunk driver suddenly careened across the middle line and smashed headlong into their car. Screams. Sirens. Ambulance. Hospital. Critical Care Unit. Endless hours. Waiting. Waiting.

Now at least twenty years later, I must confess I am

awed by Harvey's dedication. He miraculously escaped the
car crash with minor injuries. Lucille, however, became a
semi-vegetable, paralyzed from the waist down. She com-
municates in grunts and gestures. It has never been easy
since that fateful night. Harvey serves her, hand and foot,
with obvious love. It is touching to watch him bend over
and kiss her twisted lips.

Do I need to reveal his internal struggles and
temptations? I can't. My eyes are welling up with tears at
the mere thought of his faithfulness through it all. Harvey
loves right anyway.

Shelly

Shelly is a gorgeous blonde. That's the first thing
guys notice when they see her. She turns heads wherever
she goes.

At seventeen, her social calendar is filled. Her list
of accomplishments go on and on. Yearbook staff member.
Cheerleader. Student council member. And that's just the
beginning.

Shelly is different from a lot of other young women
who possess similar talent and beauty. She is a virgin and
plans to stay that way till marriage. Her future husband
will receive a precious gift—a sexually pure wife. Sure,
she's had plenty of opportunities to go out with guys who
are bent on reducing the virgin population of the country,
but she's not interested in that scene. Any date she does go
on, she sets the standards in advance. The temptation is always there, but she's not available.

In fact, she's taking the offensive in the battle.
Using Josh McDowell's "Why Wait?" books as ammunition,
she has begun a grass-roots movement in her school. She
is having a great time, and others are beginning to capture
her attitude. Personal purity without snobbish self-
righteousness. Shelly lives right anyway.

Staying Faithful

There are thousands of godly heroes who have chosen to remain faithful to God even when no one around them understands. Employees who refuse to justify their "rights" to steal time or supplies from their employers. Spiritual leaders who reject the temptation to use guilt, flattery or other impure motives to motivate their congregations to give or work. Traveling businessmen who, while away from home, refuse to see X-rated videos, to engage in telephone sex conversations or to purchase the latest issues of pornographic magazines.

You and I can be people of character in our own small ways. We can be hospitable to people without grumbling behind their backs later on. We can genuinely rejoice with someone who is excited about something new in his or her life. We can show mercy to someone who actually deserves to be pummeled into unconsciousness with an organic carrot.

Living right, *anyway*, in the small things, makes it easier to live right, *anyway*, in the bigger things.

Bert and Ferd say it's true.

Points to Ponder

1. When was the last time you were tempted to compromise in a situation? What did you do? Are you glad you did it?

2. Which scenario in this chapter do you relate to? Why?

TWELVE

Prepare for Failure, Plan for Success

It takes a steady hand to carry a full cup.
—Anonymous

C ome on down to Jones Auto. I'm overstocked on my inventory of new cars and trucks and have to move them out by the 31st of this month."

The camera pans a long line of shiny vehicles while the TV salesman talks to me with enthusiasm and fervor. Balloons, streamers and pretty women are spaced evenly throughout the scene. There I sit in my favorite living room chair, viewing the action-packed commercial from the comforts of my own home. There is something about his presentation that touches a cynical nerve.

"Take advantage of the situation. My back is against the wall. Ignore the sticker—let's dicker. I'm putting you in the driver's seat."

I turn to my wife, sounding like a self-proclaimed authority on the subject of advertising and marketing, "It's a numbers game. Probably less than one percent of the entire viewing audience will actually think that they can take advantage of him and get a cheaper price."

"Hmmm," my wife responds, allowing me to feel like I have arrived at a stunning insight. Fueled by that, I begin to think about the implications of what I have just said.

Everyone loves to take advantage of a vulnerable situation. Aren't you attracted to fire sales, We've-lost-our-lease sales, and We're-moving-so-everything-must-go sales? We might get something real cheap at someone else's expense. Admit it. Both you and I are opportunists.

Failure and the Opportunist

One of the greatest fears you and I may possess is the fear of failure. Failure is inevitable. It is a fact of life. No matter how much we use the "P" word — *plan* — Murphy's Law goes into effect: *If anything can go wrong, it will.* That's why we need to prepare properly for failure. Athletes. Business professionals. Blue collar workers. We all need to budget failure into the account of our minds.

What is so fearful about failure? We feel out of control. Vulnerable. Easy pickings. Buzzard bait. We know too much about opportunists and how they function, because we are one. *What are they going to think about me? What are they saying about me behind my back?* We know our own judgmental thought patterns toward others and we tend to assume they feel the same way about us.

What makes it even more difficult is that most of us aren't sure about God's feelings toward us when we fail either. So we tend to believe He has rejected us as well. We can almost hear Him saying, "What a poor excuse for a human being. I've lost my patience. No more chances for that loser!"

It doesn't stop there, though, because Satan isn't standing idly by, twiddling his thumbs. We know that he is the ultimate opportunist. In Isaiah 14 it says that when

Lucifer is kicked into hell forever, the people will squint their eyes in disbelief and say, "Are you the skinny little runt that weakened the nations and caused such an international stir? Where is your pomp and splendor now?"

Satan's poker hand is tipped for all to see. His strategy is to weaken people till they lose their strength and then he takes advantage of the situation. Just take a long look at world history. Every empire, whether it was Greece, Rome, Assyria or Babylonia, was destroyed by internal influences long before it crumbled by measurable standards.

Take a peek at your life. Haven't personal discouragement and disillusionment been some of the greatest monsters you've had to conquer in your world? Maybe you're in that battle right now.

God, however, has a special military strategy that makes the devil play right into His hands. Knowing that Satan preys upon weak, unguarded victims, God, in turn, takes advantage of Satan's tactics to bring praise to Himself. Remember, He is in the business of redeeming seemingly impossible situations.

Biblical "Failures"

As I am writing, a few biblical illustrations pop into my mind.

Remember Ai? The nation of Israel had just come off a tremendous victory at Jericho. The sixth chapter of Joshua chronicles the drama complete with dusty marches, trumpet blasts and crumbling walls. After such a defeat, the Israelites got cocky and sent only several thousand troops to Ai, proclaiming a leisurely triumph in advance. Not so!

The soldiers from Ai slaughtered thirty-six of the Israelites and forced the rest of the army into a panicky retreat. Joshua pleaded with God to tell the reason for such an upset. All fingers pointed to Achan, a soldier who had hidden forbidden booty in his tent. The sin in the camp was dealt with and then God instructed Joshua to implement an unusual scheme.

Thirty thousand men were instructed to hide themselves behind Ai under the cover of night. Another 5,000 were commanded to lie in wait on the west side of the city. The next morning Joshua and the rest of the women, children and men of war moved the entire camp to the north of Ai, in clear view of the city. Even though there was a valley between, they looked completely vulnerable. So much so that the king of Ai, the consummate opportunist, saw an easy conquest. His whole army quickly assembled on the plain. He yelled, "Charge!"

Joshua and the entire camp pretended they were already beaten and began to retreat into the wilderness. Cecil B. DeMille, the famous filmmaker, would have loved this plot. Intensity. High drama. Conflict. The bad guys were winning. The good guys were between a rock and a hard place. The entire nation was about to be wiped out. OH NO!

All of a sudden the seemingly defenseless Israelites stopped and turned to face the rapidly approaching enemy. Joshua lifted his spear. It flashed in the early morning sunlight. At that signal the men in hiding converged upon the city with a mighty shout and set it on fire. The Aites looked to the rear, the front, the right and the left. They were completely surrounded by trained Israelite warriors. That day 12,000 of the enemy were slaughtered and God's people were victorious.

Apparent weakness and vulnerability were used as ploys to defeat the foe. The army from Ai, being ruthlessly opportunistic by nature, was attracted to weakness. That was their downfall.

Let's take a look at another time Israel routed the

enemy under similar conditions. Second Kings 3 paints the picture.

Once again, the nation of Israel was in trouble—up to their tails in alligators. Mesha, the King of Moab, had revolted and had refused to pay tribute to Israel in the form of 100,000 sheep and wool from 100,000 rams. Joram, King of Israel, caught wind of the rebellious plan and mobilized his troops along with those from Judah and Edom. The plan was to cross the Desert of Edom and attack the Moabites to let them know in no uncertain terms who was still in power.

After a roundabout march of seven days, the troops were thirsty and demoralized—with no water for them or their animals. Things were certainly looking bleak. They decided to pitch their tents and stay for a while.

The prophet Elisha was summoned and he prophesied, saying, "Dig a bunch of ditches in this valley today. You won't see any rain or feel any wind, but tomorrow morning there will be so much water that you'll hardly know what to do with it all." The rest of the day was spent digging holes in the ground.

Sure enough, the next morning water was everywhere around the camp. Meanwhile, sensing the Israelite's apparent vulnerability, the Moabites had gathered nearby. The Moabite soldiers whispered hoarsely in the misty darkness. It was almost dawn. Within the hour the peaked roofs of the Israelite tents were discernable. The sun emerged gloriously over the gently rolling hills, cutting the murkiness with brilliant rays.

"Look," proclaimed a swordsman in a sort of stage whisper, "That's blood! Those kings have slaughtered each other! The water is all bloody! Can you see it?" The message was communicated excitedly up and down the ranks. Everyone concurred. There must have been a civil war during the night.

Little did he or the rest of the troops realize that the sun was merely shining upon the water at such an angle as to give the appearance of blood.

The King of Moab gave the signal. The entire army stealthily advanced toward the ghostly encampment. As they drew closer it seemed as though their suspicions were verified. The precise, cautious movement now turned into a casual sort of march with swords hung loosely by relaxed sides. This was going to be easy pickings! They even started talking, laughing and boasting.

All of a sudden Israelite, Edomite and Judean soldiers leaped out of their tents — ferocious and ready to fight. Within short order most of the Moabites were slaughtered and the rest were chased over hill and dale.

Different story. Same principle. The opportunistic nature of the Moabites was lured toward that which seemed to be unguarded, exposed — vulnerable. It was that attraction God sovereignly used to ensure their defeat.

The Ultimate "Failure"

Are you beginning to understand the strategy God uses to fight many of His enemies? Remember, you and God are a majority no matter how weak you feel. He specializes in using those who don't have it all together. When the powers of evil seem to be winning, He sets an ambush. And He's included you a victory that was won almost 2,000 years ago. Let's take a fresh look at that event.

The greatest battle ever fought was initiated with the birth of a tiny baby boy — a most vulnerable being. Even though the war had been declared in the Garden of Eden, the final battle started in the humble surroundings of a cattle shed.

Can you imagine the devil's sardonic response? "C'mon God! What are You trying to do, insult my intelligence? A baby? You've got to be kidding! I can destroy Him in a flash. After all, I was the one who invaded Your perfect little utopia at the Garden of Eden. Ever since that time I have warped and perverted anything and everything You've ever done! And now this!"

Satan inspired Herod to have all Hebrew boys under the age of two put to death in an attempt to have Jesus killed. You know the story. Jesus was spared. Ever the consummate opportunist, Lucifer desired to take advantage of the situation later on when Jesus was fasting in the wilderness. During this perilous time, he hit the Lord with his craftiest temptations. Jesus was tempted in all points, like us, yet He remained holy and blameless — without sin. He also passed the tests of wily Pharisees, thick-headed disciples and raging mobs.

No question about it, the drama began to build in the Garden of Gethsemane. With great drops of blood coming from His pores because of anguish and with disciples slumbering during His greatest hour of need, Jesus experienced overbearing pressure. Millions of demons were on hand taking advantage of the situation, attempting to bring about a premature death.

A betrayal kiss. Beatings. Mockery. Heavy timber ripping through tender skin. Muffled thuds of hammer against spikes.

Picture the scene in your mind. It's 33 A.D., 11:55 A.M., with a hot sun overhead. Roman guards clad in weighty armor, chuckling nonchalantly in the background. But a strong, penetrating silence begins to pervade the air.

Now you see Him. A mangled, raw figure of blood-ridden flesh, hanging innocently against the sky. Suddenly it begins to grow dark. The laughter stops. A sense of fear grips the onlooking crowd. A shrill scream ushers from the undeserving victim, "My God, my God! Why hast thou forsaken me?"

No answer. Only darkness. He seems to grow still.

"It is finished," He gasps and commits His spirit to His Father. He is dead.

As 2 Corinthians 13:4 says, "He was crucified in weakness." *Astheneō* is the term used in the original language to describe His weakened condition. Here are some of its definitions: Diseased, powerless, sick, feeble and infirm. These terms describe Jesus at His crucifixion. He appeared to be an utter failure.

All the demons of hell must have been enjoying a foaming-at-the-mouth party. "Aha! Jesus, the final hope for the world, has been annihilated! No more trouble from our former Boss. We motivated His disciples to turn against Him. We whipped the crowds into a heated frenzy. Jehovah sent His best and only. And now look at Him; He's been exterminated. We have won! Yahoo!"

Little did Satan and his vile cohorts realize that they had played right into God's hand. God's age-old tactic worked because 2 Corinthians 13:4 says even though Jesus was crucified in weakness, yet He lives by God's power. The resurrection sealed Satan's doom.

Once again, God capitalized on Satan's opportunistic nature. The apparent vulnerability of Jesus, rejected and alone, was the attraction. Lucifer couldn't pass it up! This was too easy!

But out of it all came the most significant event of human history. Our faith hinges upon it. The resurrection! Hallelujah! Doesn't that make you absolutely excited? The devil has been defeated once and for all!

No ABC Plan

I can, however, hear somebody in a snake-filled, murky swamp groaning, "Yeah, but how does all this stuff about the Aites, the Moabites and military strategies help me in my situation?" I'm so glad he asked.

Like this guy in the swamp, have you ever been surrounded by such a cloud of failure that you felt like quitting? I know I have. There have been at least a half dozen times over the years that I've written a resignation and then have read it ever so eloquently to my wife. I thank God that I've never read any of them to my congregation. Recently I dug up one that I had kept on file for posterity.

> I want to thank everyone here for all the support and kindness you have shown me and my family over the past few years. During recent months, however, I have been made painfully aware of my lack of ability to lead. The church will grow under a different style of leadership. I point no fingers at anyone but myself. You deserve better. As of this morning I am resigning as pastor of this church, even though I am willing to stay for a short while to help with the transition. Thank you for your patience with me.

Written as a true martyr. I took all the blame. As I look at the wrinkled sheet of paper in my hands, I chuckle. It all seems so far away.

Yet, I recall the circumstances surrounding this almost-resignation. A casual perusal of the old Appointment Book from that year brings a flood of memories. Sleepless nights. Indigestion. Personality clashes. Loneliness. Family and church financial worries. A series of exciting plans and then disappointments. On and on it goes.

All my education and experience didn't amount to a hill of beans. Any talent, charisma or personal ability might as well have been thrown away. None of it could pull me through this time. I felt like an absolute failure.

I had memorized enough of the Scriptures and knew enough doctrine to fill a hot air balloon, but now something was different. During this period in my life, I felt like Daniel did when he said, "I had no strength left . . . I was helpless" (Daniel 10:7-19).

Somehow, Jesus was present, waiting for me to cease trying to *work* for Him, using my own "animal heat" production. I was ready to start *knowing* Him as my life, allowing Him to be my all in all.

I can't point to any magical ABC formula that helped me through this low period or any of the others. It is just that I have, by God's grace, ultimately kept my heart open and teachable toward Jesus. He has done the rest. He has brought success.

God's Idea of Success

Even though I have studied the concept carefully, to this day I'm not sure I know the full definition of the word *success*. I do know that if we meditate upon His Word and apply scriptural principles, He promises to "make our way prosperous and then we will have good success" (Joshua 1:8).

Peter gets released from prison while James gets his head cut off. Who was more successful? I believe that both were in the center of God's will and, therefore, both were successful.

Herein lies the key. *If we continue trusting God and remaining pure in the midst of failure, God will reward us with a new level of inner stability and maturity. That's success by His standards.* If, however, we use the negative aspects of our circumstances as excuses for backsliding, grumbling or quitting, we are merely prolonging the inevitable. God will continue to probe the condition of our hearts with various and sundry circumstances until we confront our disguised pride and receive His mercy.

Bluntly put, *failure is inevitable.* It will rear its ugly head when you least expect it. Even when things are going well, the fear of it can creep up so that you can't enjoy yourself or your pleasant circumstances.

Prepare for failure in advance by actively trusting God in every detail of your life. Cultivate the attitude of gratitude. Learn to sing psalms, hymns and spiritual songs—making melody in your heart. Retain your sense of humor. Actually giggle when you catch yourself experiencing minor flashes of neurosis. Meditate on Scripture. Be careful of the type of music you listen to and the types of programs you watch on television. Remember: GIGO (Garbage In, Garbage Out).

Plan for success. In the midst of failure you will marvel at the sovereign plans God uses to ambush that old yellow-bellied sap sucker, the devil. Satan is already defeated. He will be sabotaged at every point.

Success will come. That's not a threat—it's a promise. In the darkest hour you will sense, like never before, maturity and godly authority residing in your soul. God will reward your faithful endurance. Your confidence and poise will be enhanced. Your prayer life will take on a new dimension. Your witness will be sharpened. Your counsel will be in demand.

Bert and Ferd urge you to prepare for failure, but plan for success.

Points to Ponder

1. Do you fear a potential failure in an area of your life right now? How can you disarm it, using the suggestions in this chapter?

2. Can you think of a time when you felt vulnerable in a situation, only to see the problem resolved to your advantage? Do you think God arranged it this way? How did this experience affect your faith?

3. Can you picture Satan as a defeated foe? What does the cross of Jesus mean to you?

4. What is your definition of success? How does that definition match up with the counsel of Scripture?

THIRTEEN

Elevator Express

We have all eternity to rejoice in victories won,
but only a small period of time
in which to win them.
— C. T. Studd

KAPOW! The car rocked forward sharply, snapping my head back on the headrest. Before proceeding through a four-way intersection I had been waiting for a car coming from the left to complete it's turn. I had looked up in my rear view mirror and had seen him coming. *He's going to hit me,* I thought. He did just that! He smacked head-on into my rear bumper doing about 8 mph.

I drove the car around the corner and parked. He followed suit. I winced, while pulling myself out of the car, at the strange, new pain that pulsated in the lower section of my back. We both met at the vacant spot between our cars, immediately inspecting the slight damage done to both vehicles.

"I'm sorry; it's my fault. Are you all right?" he offered. And then laughing nervously he added, "I hate to meet people by accident." I observed the well-dented side of his car. I wasn't the first person he had met in this manner.

We exchanged insurance information and then parted company. While driving to my destination, I noticed that normal neck and shoulder movements caused minor discomfort. I decided to play it safe and go to the hospital instead for X rays.

Four hours later, for the first time in my life, I was looking at my internal skeletal structure. It was a peculiar feeling. With great interest I inspected the curvature of the spinal column, the delicate attachments between each vertebra, and the way the cranium was balanced at the top. This was not some abstract high school anatomy project. This was me. My skull. My ribs. My spine. My neck. Fearfully and wonderfully made.

Everything seemed to be put together in such a fragile manner. I asked a few questions. The doctor answered each question thoroughly, pointing to various parts of the X rays while he talked. He assured me that even though there would be some soreness for a while, no permanent damage had been done.

The images I saw on his office wall had almost a haunting effect upon me. Even though I had considered it numerous times before, the brevity of life seemed to be more real than ever before. I went home and pondered a well-known Scripture:

> The length of our days is seventy years—or eighty, if we have the strength; yet their span is but trouble and sorrow. For they quickly pass, and we fly away . . . . Teach us to number our days aright, that we may gain a heart of wisdom (Psalm 90:10,12, NIV).

Moses wrote this psalm. He may have had an experience similar to mine that had caused him to ponder the shortness of his life. Maybe he had just survived a near wreck in his horse-drawn chariot while showing off to his wife. Possibly he had encountered a nervous, stuttering bandit on a deserted Egyptian road and had almost lost his life because he had trouble understanding the thief's demands. Or what if he had just barely escaped a brick avalanche while visiting the construction site of an enormous pyramid? Regardless of the situation, Moses was thinking about the brevity of his life, which piqued my curiosity about the subject.

I was inquisitive enough to resort to mathematics. I had flunked algebra in the 9th grade and my teacher had given me a semi-passing grade the second time around just to get rid of me. So you can see — I must've really been burning with curiosity to work with numbers on this subject. The batteries in the calculator were dead, so I found pencil and paper and began the laborious task of figuring out the number of my days.

At the time I was thirty-three years of age. My approximate calculations were based upon the premise that I would live to the age of seventy and that the rapture would not occur before that time. At the risk of sounding morbid, the following is an estimate of how much time I had left to live, barring the unknown:

Total (including sleep)	Actual (awake)
37 years left	25 waking years left
444 months left	296 waking months left
1924 weeks left	1283 waking weeks left
13,505 days left	9003 waking days left
324,120 hours left	216,084 waking hours left
19,447,200 minutes left	12,965,059 waking minutes left

Incredible! No wonder James likened our lives to that of steam rising from boiling water. Now you see it. Now you don't. No wonder King David questioned why God would even bother to waste His time with mortal beings — the confused lot that we are. In the whole scheme of things, including eternity past and eternity future, our lives are like a slight blip on a hospital monitor.

Knowing What's Ahead...

With this in clear view, permit me to reveal a pet theory of mine that may help usher some meaning into our existence: *The knowledge of future events directly affects present day decisions and priorities.* It helps us number our days.

For example, what would your response be if you were the only person on the planet who knew beyond the shadow of a doubt that the price of gold was going to double on the first of next month?

Sure, this is a hypothetical situation and it is highly unlikely that you or I would ever be privy to such information, but come along for the ride. Imagine with me for a few moments. Would you consider buying as much gold as you could afford? How about borrowing some money, setting a pay back deadline with interest for the fifth day of next month? It is the rare individual that would totally disregard this type of opportunity to make a quick profit on a legitimate investment.

I guarantee that the knowledge of a sudden upsurge in the price of gold would have a direct impact on the priorities and decisions made during the days before that event.

Consider another plane. What about the biblical reality of future events? Rapture. Anti-Christ. Armageddon. Great White Throne Judgment. Millennium.

Pause for a few moments. Look around you. Are you in a public setting? Perhaps an airport or a restaurant? Are you all alone — snug as a bug in a rug at your home or office?

Regardless of who is or is not around you, let out a long, luxurious yawn — complete with a lazy groan. Stretch. Close your eyelids for several seconds and try to picture in your mind's eye the last elevator you rode in.

You are the only person in the elevator. You push the button marked Lower Level and the split doors rumble shut. The suspended carriage begins its steady descent. Sighing, you glance at your watch. For once you're early for an appointment. You strike your customary elevator pose — standing erect, looking straight ahead at the middle crack between the doors with an occasional upward view of the ever-changing, lighted level indicators. You wait. And wait.

You become a tad nervous. The normal span of time has long since elapsed. An eerie feeling grips the pit of your stomach. You instinctively scrutinize the lighted indicator, but it is stationary. The hum of the elevator, however, is still present. There's an awkward, out-of-control moment while the subconscious part of your mind bombards the conscious with every fear, suspicion or worry that it can conjure up.

You try gallantly to regain emotional control. After another minute ticks by, though, there is a growing realization that you are in some kind of Twilight Zone experience. You pick up the elevator phone, tapping the cradle. It's dead. Frantically, you push the stop button. Nothing happens. You are still moving steadily downward. You begin to pummel the doors with your fists until the sudden influx of adrenalin has been drained. No response. No hope.

You fall to the floor in an exhausted heap. You are perspiring. It's warm in the cubicle — warmer than usual. All of a sudden the elevator grinds to a halt. The whirring has ceased. No noise can be heard, other than the thump-thump-thump of your heart. You reach out frantically, attempting to pry the doors apart. "Ouch!" Quickly you draw back from the heat.

At that instant, the doors open to reveal the most hideous creature you have ever seen. It is more evil than your worst nightmare. Green, scaly skin with odd tufts of hair all over. Hands that look like eagle talons. Sinister markings on its face, with bushy eyebrows. Bright yellow eyes with a single black spot in each that seem to penetrate right through you. You cower in the corner. Words cannot explain the terror that is surging through your body.

"Come with me," it says in a garbled voice. It turns, walking away with a jerky sort of shuffle. You hesitate for a moment. You feel helpless. You obey out of fear for the consequences of non-compliance.

Sights, sounds and smells assault your senses as you walk nine or ten steps behind it. The acrid odor of burning sulphur irritates your nostrils. The cacophony of shrieks and groans grows louder and louder. You look around at all the ghostly shapes and forms. It's pitch black, yet you can see everything in muted tones because of the red glowing stuff on both sides of the rough path.

The creature turns a corner and opens a creaking door, revealing a huge domed cavern that is at least fifty miles across. Stalactites hang precariously from the ceiling. The heat is overwhelming. Instinctively, you shield your face and enter cautiously. Before you have a chance to view the entire picture, you hear desperate voices moaning. It sends cold shivers pulsating up and down your spine. They are calling your name in the most pitiful manner. Their cries for help leave you speechless.

Still attempting to protect your facial skin with your arm, you look around at a most wretched scene. A molten lava-type substance is set at a rolling boil. Bubbling. Gurgling. Gently popping.

Thousands of arms are waving, with bodies bobbing in the thick, red liquid. Famous and infamous names etched on metallic collars are attached to various ghoulish-looking souls. You recognize these people. Some are from ancient history. You remembered studying about them in school. Some are from more recent history. And some are people you actually know. Frightening. You turn your head away in horror.

"Let me leave. Please, let me go. I can't stand it any longer," you plead with the demon. He pauses dramatically and then obliges with a leering grin. The gateway screeches shut behind you. A hundred questions flood your mind as you follow. *Where are we going? Why was the creature waiting for me? How does it know me? Why am I here? I know how I got here, but . . . but, how did I get here?*

Your pulse quickens. There's the elevator! It's almost too good to be true! The brute stops in front of the entrance and then steps to one side inviting you to enter. You do so. The doors close behind you before you have a chance to turn around. You push the button marked Upper Level. Refreshingly, it responds.

Relief! You sink to the floor, face in hands, not caring who sees you or how you look. You just sit there, leaning against the back wall with legs sprawled out.

Minutes pass. You are still in a daze. You think about what you have just seen. You shudder as the impact of it all slowly settles in your mind. The heebee jeebees run up and down your spine again. It all happened so quickly. But did it *really* happen? Maybe this is just a dream. No answer. You've lost all track of time. It doesn't seem to really matter, somehow.

Your disjointed thoughts are interrupted by abrupt silence. Nothing is moving. You stand up, trying to reorient yourself. Suddenly the doors glide open and you are met with the most bedazzling light you have ever seen. In spite of its intensity you are not blinded by its brilliance. Your eyes look into the gentle gaze of an angelic being standing in front of you. You step off the elevator.

The first words that pop into your mind are *Glory, Honor and Power Are Due Unto Him.* Your heart is fairly bursting with praise, worship and thankfulness. All self-consciousness has evaporated. For the first time in your life you actually feel unconditionally loved, forgiven and accepted all at the same time. You are in complete harmony with your environment.

You take a few steps and then stop, attempting to capture the essence and beauty of your surroundings. The angel stands by patiently as you crane your neck, looking above and all around. The splendor of the buildings takes your breath away. They rise up for miles, farther than the eye can see. Fluffy patches of clouds. Rich, botanical gardens are everywhere filled with exotic flowers and bushes. Jewels and precious metals glint in the ever-present light.

It strikes you as unusual. There are no shadows. Three-dimensional concepts don't apply here. Buildings sort of hang together, allowing for a distinctively stunning, free flowing style of architecture. There is a thick transparent wall, over 200 feet thick, on the perimeter.

The spectrum of colors is unfathomable. Each hue emits harmonic tones of music. The angel suddenly interrupts your reverie. "Welcome," he offers. "My name is Lukas. I've been expecting you. How about a quick tour?"

Without waiting for an answer, the ministering spirit starts walking across the open expanse of the gold-tiled mall. Instinctively, you follow. You go through a series of doorways and corridors and finally you enter an immense hall.

Here, you are told, is the place where the rewards

are handed out. You are awestruck as the angel explains
the reward system. You are shown a display case with
hundreds of ornate crowns mounted in it. Suddenly a pure
zeal to win as many of those crowns as possible begins to
burn in your bosom.

You soon discover the metabolic makeup of celestial
bodies. They are constructed of an actual substance called
faith and are energized by a life principle called *love*. It is
explained that there is a hierarchy in heaven signified by
the degree of glory that glows from each body. The angelic
being mentions that the faithfulness and integrity on earth
determines the amount of light that shines from the body
in heaven. Glory in its different degrees is the garment
worn by everybody.

Time is not existent here. Everything that was — *is*.
And everything that will be — *is*, also. You are living in the
eternal *is*. It feels vibrant. Alive. You experience it, but
couldn't explain it if you tried.

Lukas touches your shoulder and in a heartbeat you
are transported with him through walls, floors and doors.
Before you can catch your breath and realize what is happening you find yourself in a most magnificent setting.

Before you is a crystal clear river flowing down the
middle of a wide, golden street. On either side of the river
stands a tree with green leaves and colorful fruit. Your gaze
follows the river to its source. There it is! The throne of
God! You feel yourself weaken. You lose control, falling flat
on your face as a dead person.

You have no idea how long you've been lying there.
Lukas bends over, gently grasping your arm. In an instant
you are flying with him, knowing not where. Not really
caring. Everything is blissful.

The next thing you comprehend is a strangely
familiar creak and groan from the elevator on its tortuous

descent. It stops. You quickly pick yourself off the floor. And not a moment too soon. The doors open and you are rudely thrust back into something you used to call reality.

A bespeckled man in a sharply tailored, pin-striped, high-authority suit with white shirt and red tie greets you at the door. As you make a stumbling exit he glances nervously at his watch, muttering something about a long wait for the elevator as he brushes past.

As I try to extricate my tongue from my cheek, think for a moment about what you've just read.

What if you had an elevator ride that allowed you to spend five minutes in heaven and five minutes in hell? What if you then returned back to earth? How would your life be changed?

Let's take a fresh look at my theory: *The knowledge of future events directly affects present day decisions and priorities.* It helps us number our days.

I am convinced of one thing. When we actually go to heaven, a sobering thing will take place when we see its majesty. We will wish that we had been more courageous and more in love with Jesus when we were on earth.

If Bert and Ferd could talk, they'd say, "Let's change that, beginning right now."

Points to Ponder

1. Does it scare you to think of your own mortality? What do you hope to accomplish before you die? Does it line up with what Scripture says is important?

2. Imagine you had the elevator experience described in this chapter. Would you make any changes in your life?

3. How can the knowledge of future events affect your present day decisions and priorities?

FOURTEEN

In Times of Need

If I had 300 men who feared nothing but God,
hated nothing but sin and were determined to know
nothing among men but Jesus Christ and Him
crucified, I would set the world on fire.
—John Wesley

What does it take for you to shrink from God? When
you fail, do you retreat and withdraw into your little
shell?

I am reminded of the challenges I encountered when
potty-training my puppy Perro. More than once I opened
the door, nose first, and immediately whiffed the distinct
odor of puppy "doo-doo" in the hallway. One time, after
carefully stepping over the smelly mess, I caught sight of
the much-too-cute, furry perpetrator of the crime. The guilt
in his eyes telegraphed to me that he knew in no uncertain
terms that where he had deposited his little "gift" was a
place contrary to the endless hours of previous instruction.

He looked at me. Then his eyes searched under the
sofa for a safe spot to hide and he furtively cast a sidelong
glance back in my direction. As he beat a hasty retreat, I
grabbed the rolled-up newspaper that had been carefully
folded to the precise specifications outlined in the puppy

training manual. Kneeling to the ground, I reached under the couch, gently pulling his unwilling frame toward me.

He was whimpering in my arms and trembling as we walked back to the scene of his crime. In a stern voice, with clenched teeth, I scolded him. "Bad boy! Naughty puppy!"

I pointed over to the newspaper lying in the corner, "Perro, I've told you a million times to go on the paper, not on the floor."

Awhumpa. Awhumpa. He yelped as the tattered paper cylinder came down upon his rear end. After taking him over to the newspaper on the floor, after lecturing him about the merits of obedience and after cleaning up the mess, I sat down on the couch in the living room, cradling him in my arms. As my voice softened with comforting words, the mischievous glint returned to his eyes. He licked my face and fervently wagged his semibushy tail. He didn't have to run and hide. The discipline was in the past. We were still friends.

Approaching the Throne of God

Many years have passed since those days, yet I can't shake off some principles that came to mind. What happened in the hallway and under the sofa is a clear-cut story of what happens to many of us in our relationship with Jesus Christ.

Over the years, we develop the concept that our performance in life dictates whether or not we can strut up to the Throne of God with boldness and confidence. Like Perro, with his tail stuffed between his legs, we tend to withdraw, trying to hide when our performance level falls beneath our concept of heaven's minimum standards.

The Scriptures, however, reveal an approach that is very different from our human experience. Let's take a windshield tour.

On the surface, the book of Leviticus appears to be a dry, old and crusty bit of literature filled with all kinds of ceremonial laws and sacrifices. Those sacrifices, though, exhibit a wonderful picture of redemption. In fact, the theme of Leviticus says an exciting mouthful: Unholy people can approach a holy God.

In the Garden of Eden we begin to see God's passion for fellowship with human beings. He creates Adam and Eve and talks with them daily. After the Fall, He takes Enoch home to heaven because of their communion together. He calls Abraham his friend. He speaks directly to Moses and even gives him glimpses of Himself. God facilitates easy access to Himself.

God then gave Moses the pattern for a tabernacle—the place where God would reveal His will in the Holy of Holies, above the mercy seat, between the outstretched wings of the golden cherubim. As history moved on Solomon's temple was built to replace the mobile tabernacle.

That temple was destroyed by the Babylonians in 587 B.C. and later rebuilt by Zerubbabel and Jews returning from Babylonian exile, only to be demolished by Titus of Rome (70 A.D.).

The temple was a symbol of God's accessibility. He wanted people to know that He was present, available to assist in times of trouble.

In the New Testament, God chose the fulfillment of all previous symbols to reveal His accessibility—His son, Jesus Christ. Through Him we enter into the Holy of Holies, the very presence of God.

God is approachable. Even in all His majesty and power, He invites us to come and fellowship with Him. There is a verse that says it all:

> Let us then approach the throne of grace with con-
> fidence, so that we may receive mercy and find grace to
> help in our time of need (Hebrews 4:16, NIV).

Three principles leap out at me as I read this passage. The first has to do with confidence. The Greek term
parrhesia[1] denotes boldness, openness and cheerful
courage. After understanding the fear of the Lord as outlined in the chapter "Rock of Jell-O," the bold approach
that God grants us is almost unbelievable. Yet the invitation to come running up to the throne of grace is abundant-
ly warm and clear.

The second concept that strikes me has to do with
the last five words, *in our time of need.* In times of need we
are not thinking pretty thoughts, saying pretty words, nor
are we making pretty decisions. Our consciences aren't
squeaky clean. I'm sure glad it doesn't say *in our time of
victory.*

Most people have been seduced into thinking that
they can strut up to the throne only when they have been
obedient and victorious. The boldness of their access is con-
ditional, based entirely upon their performance. This
produces a works-oriented, emotionally-based, roller
coaster type of existence.

When people, however, capture the essence of what
Christ meant when He said, "It is finished," liberty from a
works system and freedom from the authority of the world,
the flesh and the devil become precious. The veil covering
the Holy of Holies ripped right down the middle, providing
unrestrained access to the mercy seat. Do we dare celebrate
the meaning of all this?

Are you distraught with your performance as of
late? Do you feel like you are one hair's breadth away from
insanity? Have you recently been wondering whether or
not God is losing His patience with you? If so, you are in a

time of need. Christ has given you the go-ahead sign. You can enter His throne room with dignity right now. No hat-in-hand, down-cast eyes approach for you! It's boldness in your time of need! He is just a prayer away.

The third principle that blesses me has to do with God's grace. After all, it is the throne of grace to which we've been called.

The essence of grace is that God is for us. What's more, He is for us who, in ourselves, are against Him. More still, He is not for us merely in general attitude, but continues to effectively act for us with our benefit in mind. Grace is summed up in the person and work of Jesus Christ.

Grace can only act positively toward people who are guilty, unworthy sinners. Righteousness that has been established by human standards doesn't even get a nod from grace. So, if you're painfully aware of your need, you're a prime candidate for the throne of grace. It's the type of grace that gives you enabling power so that you will not repeatedly stumble in the same weaknesses. And it's yours for the asking.

Our Heart's Inclination

The secret to living with your conscience without going crazy is found in the word *inclination*. If your inner capacity, known as the heart, is inclined toward God you will end up obeying Him no matter how much you may struggle with rationalization during the process.

Recently I heard Dr. David Hocking during one of his daily radio broadcasts, *The Biola Hour*. He made a statement that really caused me to ponder. He said, "I have come to the place where I believe that we can be as holy as we want to be." He meant, of course, that some people don't really want to live holy lives, so they use societal influences, circumstances and heredity as excuses for their alternative lifestyles. I agree with Dr. Hocking's assessment.

Living a life of integrity is not a call to *perfection,* but to *inclination.* Just before Joshua died at the ripe old age of 110, he commanded the nation of Israel to put away false gods and told them to "incline their hearts unto the Lord God of Israel" (Joshua 24:23). In Psalm 119:112, King David said that he had inclined his heart toward obeying God's Word to the very end.

David aptly illustrated this principle in Psalm 40:8 when he said, in effect, "God, I don't always know Your will for my life, but I'll keep listening. My heart will lean in Your direction because I delight at the prospect of obeying You and living in the center of Your will when I discover it."

What expectancy and teachability! Not only was he wanting to *hear,* but also willing to *do* whatever God commanded.

And that's the key. Our Christian experience is not some heat-of-the-moment, dramatic display of talent and ability in some 100-yard dash. We're in this for the long haul. Faithfulness, endurance and integrity for a marathon run. Spiritual stamina is a rare quality in an age that caters to individuals and institutions who want the thrills of Pentecost without the suffering of Calvary. The historical record bears out that Calvary preceded Pentecost.

It's how we finish that counts. Keeping our hearts inclined toward Jesus, even in times of dire need, provides the inner poise required to handle life's unexpected challenges.

In times of need, some people pop pills or jump from window sills. In times of need, others drop their previously held theological convictions and adopt predictable, arrogant attitudes characterized by vain philosophy and deceit.

What will your sole passion be ten years from now? Oh, I know, the rapture may occur before that time and we can't boast about tomorrow. But still, think about it. You're surrounded by casualties and dropouts—people who quit at the slightest provocation. Are you going to let the life-style of your peers slowly dilute your consecration to Him?

Is your heart inclined toward Jesus or is it inclined toward the world, the flesh and the devil? Only you can answer that question. And you must. Strip away the PR image. Pull off the masks. Boil away the excuses. It will be worth the honesty.

The bottom line is that God has provided bold, confident access to His throne of grace especially in times of need. We're in a battle for our lives. It's no time for shallow games. Let's experience the power of a clear conscience.

Now is the time to fall to our faces before the throne of grace with hearts bursting in adoration for Him, *to whom all honor and glory and power is due.*

Words worth embroidering—proudly endorsed by Bert and Ferd.

Points to Ponder

1. The last time you were in need, did you run to God or away from God? Can you picture yourself walking boldly to the throne of God after a willful failure? Memorize and personalize Hebrews 4:16.

2. Do you feel your Christianity will hold up in the "long haul" of life? List three things that frighten you about your performance in the future. Meditate on Philippians 1:6 and claim its promise.

3. If your best friend were to ask you, "What principles did you glean from this book?" how would you answer him or her?

Afterword

After reading this book, if you have not made your peace with God, there is one thing that is necessary. This one thing is more necessary than your next breath, because you are only one heartbeat away from having contentment, self-control, answers to all your "why" questions or relief from all the pain and suffering you may be experiencing at this present time. If you do not have this one thing, even what you seem to have will be taken away for all eternity. I am talking about the gift of God. Consider His gift. He gave Himself in the person of His Son.

God's compassion compelled Him to build a bridge of reconciliation to all people without regard to cost. He did not spare His own Son, Jesus Christ, who humbly took the form of a man about 2,000 years ago and satisfied every demand of perfection God required. Then, in order to satisfy the justice of God, the sins of all of us were laid upon Christ so we would not have to suffer the eternal consequences of our sins.

Jesus voluntarily suffered horrible anguish for us by being nailed to a wooden cross and dying in our place. He was buried, rose again the third day and ascended into heaven, representing the whole world with His precious blood.

He has forgiven your sins; in fact, there is nothing about your past that shocks Him. He has provided meaning for the emotional agony you have endured in your lifetime. He has exhibited His genuine friendship by dying for you, in your place, with no strings attached.

There is nothing more important than being honest about your need to receive the free gift of eternal life by inviting Jesus to come and live inside your heart. The issue is not what you can do to earn God's favor, but what He has already done for you in expressing His unconditional love to you.

Come to Him right now, just as you are, by simple faith and pray:

Dear God, thank you for sending your Son, Jesus, to die on the cross in my place for my sins. I now accept the fact that the shed blood of Jesus has cleansed me from all unrighteousness. I receive Jesus Christ into my heart as the Lord of my life. Thank you for accepting me just as I am. In Jesus' name. Amen.

If you prayed this prayer, please feel free to contact me for some helpful information about your new life in Christ. Enclose a self-addressed, stamped envelope and send it to: P.O. Box 2757, Columbia, MD 21045.

APPENDIX A

The Fear Advantage

As you have read in the chapter "Rock of Jell-O," the fear of the Lord is a vital link to understanding the connection between our human frailty and His eternal purpose for our lives in the here and now. The Bible is chock-full of promises regarding the blessing heaped upon those who fear the Lord. Place an X mark beside the benefits you desire to receive for your own life.[1]

Benefits

☐ To receive a special inheritance:
"For you have heard my vows, O God; you have given me the heritage of those who fear your name" (Psalm 61:5, NIV).

☐ To receive a greater supply of God's mercy:
"For as the heaven is high above the earth, so great is his mercy toward them that fear him" (Psalm 103:11).

☐ To live a longer life:
"The fear of the LORD adds length to life, but the years of the wicked are cut short" (Proverbs 10:27, NIV).

☐ To enjoy security for me and my family:
"He who fears the LORD has a secure fortress, and for his children it will be a refuge" (Proverbs 14:26, NIV).

☐ To experience fulfillment in life and protection from evil:
"The fear of the LORD tendeth to life: and he that hath it shall abide satisfied; he shall not be visited with evil" (Proverbs 19:23).

☐ To receive riches, respect and long life:
"Humility and the fear of the LORD bring wealth and honor

and life" (Proverbs 22:4, NIV).

☐ To overcome the lure of sin and temptation:
"By mercy and truth iniquity is purged: and by the fear of
the LORD men depart from evil" (Proverbs 16:6).

☐ To be contented:
"Better a little with the fear of the LORD than great wealth
with turmoil" (Proverbs 15:16, NIV).

☐ To start being a wise and understanding person:
"The fear of the LORD is the beginning of wisdom, and
knowledge of the Holy One is understanding" (Proverbs
9:10, NIV).

☐ To start learning the essence of knowledge:
"The fear of the LORD is the beginning of knowledge"
(Proverbs 1:7).

☐ To have God's many promises confirmed to me:
"Stablish thy word unto thy servant, who is devoted to thy
fear" (Psalm 119:38).

☐ To be rescued from danger by an angel:
"The angel of the LORD encamps around those who fear
him and he delivers them" (Psalm 34:7, NIV).

☐ To be honored by God:
"He honoureth them that fear the LORD" (Psalm 15:4).

☐ To share in the Lord's secrets:
"The LORD confides in those who fear him; he makes his
covenants known to them" (Psalm 25:14, NIV).

☐ To receive from God's storehouse of goodness:
"How great is your goodness, which you have stored up for
those who fear you, which you bestow in the sight of men"
(Psalm 31:19, NIV).

☐ To be blessed—to the point of being envied:
"Blessed are all who fear the LORD, who walk in his ways"
(Psalm 128:1, NIV).

☐ To be watched over by God:
"The eyes of the LORD are on those who fear him, on those
whose hope is in his unfailing love" (Psalms 33:18, NIV).

☐ To have all my needs supplied:
"Fear the LORD, you his saints, for those who fear him lack nothing" (Psalm 34:9, NIV).

☐ To have a teachable attitude:
"Come, my children, listen to me; I will teach you the fear of the LORD" (Psalm 34:11, NIV).

☐ To be sought out for help in times of trouble:
"But for those who fear you, you have raised a banner to be unfurled against the bow" (Psalm 60:4, NIV).

☐ To be the recipient of God's compassion:
"As a father has compassion on his children, so the LORD has compassion on those who fear him" (Psalm 103:13, NIV).

☐ To leave a legacy to my grandchildren:
"But from everlasting to everlasting the LORD's love is with those who fear him, and his righteousness with their children's children" (Psalm 103:17, NIV).

☐ To receive daily provisions:
"He provides food for those who fear him; he remembers his covenant forever" (Psalm 111:5, NIV).

☐ To have a clear focus upon eternal value:
"Do not let your heart envy sinners, but always be zealous for the fear of the LORD" (Proverbs 23:17, NIV).

☐ To have a healthy body:
"Do not be wise in your own eyes; fear the LORD and shun evil. This will bring health to your body and nourishment to your bones" (Proverbs 3:7,8, NIV).

☐ To grow in wisdom:
"The fear of the Lord teaches a man wisdom, and humility comes before honor" (Proverbs 15:33, NIV).

☐ To discover the source of life:
"The fear of the LORD is a fountain of life, turning a man from the snares of death" (Proverbs 14:27, NIV).

☐ To have God be pleased with me:
"The LORD delights in those who fear him, who put their

hope in his unfailing love" (Psalm 147:11, NIV).

☐ To be immortalized in God's book of remembrance:
"Then those who feared the LORD talked with each other,
and the LORD listened and heard. A scroll of remembrance
was written in his presence concerning those who feared
the LORD and honored his name" (Malachi 3:16, NIV).

☐ To be motivated to tell others how to be saved from hell:
"We know what it means to fear the Lord, and so we try to
persuade others" (2 Corinthians 5:11, TEV).

☐ To know my basic purpose for being alive:
"Now all has been heard; here is the conclusion of the matter: Fear God and keep his commandments, for this is the
whole duty of man. For God will bring every deed into
judgement, including every hidden thing, whether it is
good or evil" (Ecclesiastes 12:13,14, NIV).

☐ Godly desires are satisfied:
"He fulfills the desires of those who fear him; he hears their
cry and saves them" (Psalm 145:19, NIV).

What are the consequences of not fearing the Lord? Place an
X mark beside the results you want to avoid in your life:

Consequences

☐ There is a cold heart:
"Because they have no changes, therefore, they fear not
God" (Psalm 55:19, KJV).

☐ God resists me:
"Then they will call to me but I will not answer; they will
look for me but will not find me . . . [They] hated
knowledge and did not choose to fear the LORD" (Proverbs
1:28,29, NIV).

☐ Effective church discipline is bypassed:
"Them that sin rebuke before all, that others also may
fear" (1 Timothy 5:20).

☐ There is no real desire for personal holiness:
"All these promises are made to us, my dear friends. So

then, let us purify ourselves from everything that makes body or soul unclean, and let us be completely holy by living in reverence for God" (2 Corinthians 7:1, TEV).

☐ There is a disrespect for others:
"Submitting yourselves one to another in the fear of God" (Ephesians 5:21).

☐ There is need to gossip and slander:
"I will teach you the fear of the LORD. Whoever of you loves life and desires to see many good days, keep your tongue from evil and your lips from speaking lies" (Psalm 34:11-13, NIV).

☐ There is an arrogant attitude:
"To fear the LORD is to hate evil; I hate pride and arrogance, evil behavior and perverse speech" (Proverbs 8:13, NIV).

☐ There is no effective soulwinning:
"But sanctify the Lord God in your hearts: and be ready always to give an answer to every man that asketh you a reason of the hope that is in you with meekness and fear" (1 Peter 3:15).

☐ God's rest seems to be unattainable:
"Let us therefore fear, lest a promise being left us of entering into his rest, any of you should seem to come short of it" (Hebrews 4:1).

☐ There is an obsession for temporal security and approval:
"Since you call on a Father who judges each man's work impartially, live your lives as strangers here in reverent fear" (1 Peter 1:17, NIV).

☐ Evil goes unrestrained:
"Their throats are open graves; their tongues practice deceit. The poison of vipers is on their lips. Their mouths are full of cursing and bitterness. Their feet are swift to shed blood; ruin and misery mark their ways, and the way of peace they do not know. There is no fear of God before their eyes" (Romans 3:13-18, NIV).

APPENDIX B

Choices

Recently I had a lot of fun playing the challenging game "CHOICES."[1] It is an adventure of thought that begins with a dilemma and ends with a choice. Feel free to use the dilemmas below for interaction with your family, class, youth group or simply for your own personal growth. You'll discover that most answers don't come easy — but that's the point of the game. You'll be face to face with life and sometimes nose to nose with opposing viewpoints. Have fun!

I thank Rainfall, Inc. for granting permission to reprint the dilemmas below and the biblical principles to help make the right choices in Appendix C.

- Your wife has made $1,000 from selling a number of her paintings which she does at home. Will you declare this money on your income tax?

- You need copies of a song for school but you don't have time to order them. Will you photocopy it even though the song is copyrighted, making photocopying illegal?

- You have a contract with a carpenter to do some work, but you found someone else who will do it much cheaper. Will you break the contract?

- You bent your car fender backing out of the garage. A week later another car hits yours in the rear. His insurance company will pay for the accident. Will you include the bent fender in the estimate to the insurance company?

- You are married with two teenage sons. You live fifteen miles away from your mother who, since learning she has

175

cancer, has given up wanting to live and needs constant care. Will you quit your job to help her?

- You have extra income from babysitting which you need to make ends meet. You are sixty-six years old and the extra income will cause you to lose social security benefits. Will you report the extra income?

- Your sixteen-year-old daughter left her diary on her desk. You have heard rumors she is seeing a boy of whom you disapprove. Will you read the diary while she is out?

- You have been invited to join an exclusive organization which could help your career, but it means cutting back on your expenses, including charitable donations. Will you join?

- You belong to a small sharing group in which members discuss mutual problems. Will you share with the group problems you have with your spouse?

- You had an argument with your spouse and he/she is not speaking to you. You believe you were in the right. Will you apologize first?

- A good friend wants to leave her husband. When he drinks heavily, he abuses her verbally and physically. They have two children, ages eight and ten. Will you advise her to leave?

- You are to be married as soon as your divorce is finalized. Will you live with your fiancé before the wedding to save expenses?

- You have been outspoken against lenient sentences for criminals. Your nineteen-year-old son was arrested for the second time for possession of marijuana. Will you hire a good lawyer in hopes of preventing your son from going to jail?

- You teach history in the high school and have been asked to lower your passing grade so the star football player can pass. Will you do it?

- Your brother-in-law slandered you at work. Because of this you missed a promotion. Your wife has asked you to forget the incident. Will you?

- Your neighbor has asked you to sign a petition to abolish the death penalty. Will you sign it?

- You are an undercover agent for the government. Will you lie to catch traitors?

- You are a missionary who takes Bibles into a communist country. Will you continue to do this even if it means lying to the border guards?

- Money is tight. You're working hard but the bills are piling up. You notice the state lottery is at an all-time high. Will you buy a ticket?

- Your teenage son wants to be a doctor and works part-time at a hospital. The job requires working every Sunday and always missing church. Do you advise him to quit?

- Your uncle is coming for dinner. Will you quickly hang the painting he gave you for Christmas, the one you packed away because you dislike it?

- Your sixteen-year-old son plans to go camping with friends, one of whom is a known homosexual. Will you agree to the trip?

- You paid an acquaintance much too low a price for an antique lamp you bought from him. You have since learned its true value. Will you pay him the additional amount?

- Your neighbor, who has always helped you when you needed him, is running for mayor. He has asked you to campaign for him. Will you help him even though you don't think he is the best qualified candidate?

- Several friends have suggested to you that you get help to curb your bad temper. You've never hurt anyone physically. Will you seek help?

- You are pregnant and tests indicate your baby will have serious defects. You are forty-seven, and your husband is fifty-five. Will you consider abortion as a solution to the problem?

- Your wife is terminally ill and very uncomfortable. You have discovered she is saving pills to take one large dose to kill herself. Will you make believe you don't know this?

- You know doctors say smoking is bad for you, but it is so hard to quit. Everyone has some vices. Will you keep smoking?

- Will you tell your spouse about a brief affair you had that is now finished?

- You never miss work unless you are very sick, but most of the other employees aren't so conscientious. Will you follow their example and call in sick when you just want a day off?

- You are promoted over another employee because you had seniority. You later find out that the records are wrong and the other employee has more seniority than you. Will you tell your boss?

- Your nineteen-year-old son works and pays you room and board, but his lifestyle is opposite to yours, including smoking marijuana. Will you tell him to leave your house?

- You are the owner of several retail stores to whom a salesman has sold stolen goods at a significant discount. You are the only one who knows this. Will you report him?

- A fellow employee has a vile tongue which is very offensive to you. You have approached him about this, but to no avail. Will you speak to your employer about this?

- You are an unemployed teacher. Jobs are hard to find in your field. Will you take a low paying, low prestige job to avoid going on welfare?

- You do a lot of extras at work including unpaid overtime, but the boss never shows his appreciation. You're tempted to use some office supplies, like stamps, for your personal use. Will you do this?

- Your tax accountant has shown you how to pay less taxes. It's not illegal but on the borderline of being unethical. Will you do it?

APPENDIX C

Twenty Choices That Are Always Right!

The following are choices that can always be made with integrity along with biblical references to support each principle.

1. CHOOSE GOD

God is true; He's right for you.

"I am the LORD your God . . . You shall have no other gods besides me" (Exodus 20:2,3, NIV).

"In all your ways acknowledge him and he will make your paths straight" (Proverbs 3:6, NIV).

"Love the LORD your God with all your heart and with all your soul and with all your mind. This is the first and greatest commandment" (Matthew 22:37, NIV).

"If you love me, you will obey what I command" (John 14:15, NIV).

2. CHOOSE LOVE

Above all, love all.

"Love never fails" (1 Corinthians 13:8, NIV).

"Love your neighbor as yourself" (Matthew 22:39, NIV).

"Do everything in love" (1 Corinthians 16:14, NIV).

"My command is this: Love each other as I have loved you" (John 15:12, NIV).

"Love does no harm to its neighbor" (Romans 13:10, NIV).

"Above all, love each other deeply, because love covers over a multitude of sins" (1 Peter 4:8, NIV).

3. CHOOSE GOOD OVER BAD

Put right in the light.

"Turn from evil and do good" (Psalm 34:14, NIV).

"Never tire of doing what is right" (2 Thessalonians 3:13, NIV).

"Hate what is evil; cling to what is good" (Romans 12:9, NIV).

"Do not be overcome by evil, but overcome evil with good" (Romans 12:21, NIV).

"Wealth is worthless in the day of wrath, but righteousness delivers from death" (Proverbs 11:4, NIV).

"Those who lead many to righteousness [will shine] like the stars for ever and ever" (Daniel 12:3, NIV).

"He who pursues righteousness and love finds life, prosperity and honor" (Proverbs 21:21, NIV).

4. CHOOSE TRUTH

Do what's true—and say it too!

"The LORD detests lying lips, but he delights in men who are truthful" (Proverbs 12:22, NIV).

"Do not lie to each other" (Colossians 3:9, NIV).

"I have chosen the way of truth; I have set my heart on your laws" (Psalm 119:30, NIV).

"These are the things you are to do: Speak the truth to each other, and render true and sound judgment in your courts" (Zechariah 8:16, NIV).

"Truthful lips endure forever, but a lying tongue lasts only a moment" (Proverbs 12:19, NIV).

5. CHOOSE OBEDIENCE

Obey today and watch it pay.

"Listen, my son, to your father's instruction and do not forsake your mother's teaching. They will be a garland to grace your head and chain to adorn your neck" (Proverbs 1:8,9, NIV).

"Children, obey your parents" (Ephesians 6:1, NIV).

"The wise in heart accept commands, but a chattering fool comes to ruin" (Proverbs 10:8, NIV).

"He who scorns instruction will pay for it, but he who respects a command is rewarded" (Proverbs 13:13, NIV).

"Peter and the other apostles replied: 'We must obey God rather than men!'" (Acts 5:29)

"Obey your leaders and submit to their authority . . . Obey them so that their work will be a joy, not a burden, for that would be of no advantage to you" (Hebrews 13:17, NIV).

6. CHOOSE FAITH

Faith and trust: a definite must.

"Trust in the LORD with all your heart and lean not on your own understanding" (Proverbs 3:5, NIV).

"Faith is being sure of what we hope for and certain of what we do not see" (Hebrews 11:1, NIV).

"Have faith in God" (Mark 11:22, NIV).

"When I am afraid, I will trust in you" (Psalm 56:3, NIV).

"Trust in the LORD forever, for the LORD, the LORD, is the Rock eternal" (Isaiah 26:4, NIV).

7. CHOOSE KINDNESS

Keep kind in mind.

"Blessed is he who is kind to the needy" (Proverbs 14:21, NIV).

"Love is kind. It does not envy, it does not boast, it is not proud. It is not rude" (1 Corinthians 13:4,5, NIV).

"An anxious heart weighs a man down, but a kind word cheers him up" (Proverbs 12:25, NIV).

"As God's chosen people, holy and dearly loved, clothe yourselves with compassion, kindness, humility, gentleness and patience" (Colossians 3:12, NIV).

"A righteous man cares for the needs of his animal, but the kindest acts of the wicked are cruel" (Proverbs 12:10, NIV).

8. CHOOSE WISDOM

Hold wisdom tight and you'll be all right.

"Wisdom is supreme; therefore, get wisdom!" (Proverbs 4:7, NIV).

"Those who are wise will shine like the brightness of the heavens" (Daniel 12:3, NIV).

"He who gets wisdom loves his own soul; he who cherishes understanding prospers" (Proverbs 19:8, NIV).

"If any of you lacks wisdom, he should ask God, who gives generously to all without finding fault, and it will be given to him" (James 1:5, NIV).

"A man is praised according to his wisdom, but men with warped minds are despised" (Proverbs 12:8, NIV).

9. CHOOSE FRIENDSHIP

The friends you choose help you win or lose.

"He who walks with the wise grows wise, but a companion of fools suffers harm" (Proverbs 13:20, NIV).

"Do not make friends with a hot-tempered man, do not associate with one easily angered, or you may learn his ways and get yourself ensnared" (Proverbs 22:24,25, NIV).

"Do not be misled: Bad company corrupts good character" (1 Corinthians 15:33, NIV).

"A friend loves at all times" (Proverbs 17:17, NIV).

"A perverse man stirs up dissension, and a gossip separates close friends" (Proverbs 16:28, NIV).

10. CHOOSE PEACE

Release peace and increase.

"Seek peace and pursue it" (Psalm 34:14, NIV).

"Live in harmony with one another" (Romans 12:16, NIV).

"Let us therefore make every effort to do what leads to peace" (Romans 14:19, NIV).

"Let the peace of Christ rule in your hearts" (Colossians 3:15, NIV).

"A gentle answer turns away wrath, but a harsh word stirs up anger" (Proverbs 15:1, NIV).

"Hatred stirs up dissension, but love covers over all wrongs" (Proverbs 10:12, NIV).

"A heart at peace gives life to the body, but envy rots the bones" (Proverbs 14:30, NIV).

11. CHOOSE STRENGTH

Hold on, be strong!

"Finally, be strong in the Lord and in his mighty power" (Ephesians 6:10, NIV).

"Do not withhold good from those who deserve it when it is in your power to act" (Proverbs 3:27, NIV).

"My flesh and my heart may fail, but God is the strength of my heart and my portion forever" (Psalm 73:26, NIV).

"Strengthen the feeble hands, steady the knees that give way; say to those with fearful hearts, 'Be strong, do not fear'" (Isaiah 35:3, NIV).

12. CHOOSE HARD WORK

Stand tall and give it your all.

"Serve wholeheartedly, as if you were serving the Lord, not men, because you know that the Lord will reward everyone for whatever good he does, whether he is slave or free" (Ephesians 6:7,8, NIV).

"In everything [Hezekiah] undertook . . . he sought his God and worked wholeheartedly. And so he prospered" (2 Chronicles 31:21, NIV).

"Laziness brings on deep sleep, and the shiftless man goes hungry" (Proverbs 19:15, NIV).

"If a man will not work, he shall not eat" (2 Thessalonians 3:10, NIV).

"He who works his land will have abundant food, but he who chases fantasies lacks judgment" (Proverbs 12:11, NIV).

13. CHOOSE GENEROSITY

The best part of living is loving and giving.

"He who gives to the poor will lack nothing, but he who closes his eyes to them receives many curses" (Proverbs 28:27, NIV).

"If [a person's gift] is contributing to the needs of others, let him give generously" (Romans 12:8, NIV).

"Share with God's people who are in need. Practice hospitality" (Romans 12:13, NIV).

"A generous man will prosper; he who refreshes others will himself be refreshed" (Proverbs 11:25, NIV).

"If a man shuts his ears to the cry of the poor, he too will cry out and not be answered" (Proverbs 21:13, NIV).

14. CHOOSE PURITY

Purity's right, day and night.

"I will maintain my righteousness and never let go of it" (Job 27:6, NIV).

"Even a child is known by his actions, by whether his conduct is pure and right" (Proverbs 20:11, NIV).

"The Lord detests the thoughts of the wicked, but those of the pure are pleasing to him" (Proverbs 15:26, NIV).

"Keep yourself pure" (1 Timothy 5:22, NIV).

"Avoid every kind of evil" (1 Thessalonians 5:22, NIV).

15. CHOOSE JUSTICE

Light the flare for fair.

"Do nothing out of favoritism" (1 Timothy 5:21, NIV).

"It is not good to be partial to the wicked or to deprive the innocent of justice" (Proverbs 18:5, NIV).

"Evil men do not understand justice, but those who seek the LORD understand it fully" (Proverbs 28:5, NIV).

Whoever says to the guilty, 'You are innocent'—people will curse him and nations denounce him. But it will go well with those who convict the guilty, and rich blessings will come upon them" (Proverbs 24:24,25, NIV).

16. CHOOSE SELF-CONTROL

Stay off the shelf; control yourself!

"Be self-controlled and alert" (1 Peter 5:8, NIV).

"Like a city whose walls are broken down is a man who lacks self-control" (Proverbs 25:28, NIV).

"A fool gives full vent to his anger, but a wise man keeps himself under control" (Proverbs 29:11, NIV).

"He who guards his mouth and his tongue keeps himself from calamity" (Proverbs 21:23, NIV).

"A man of knowledge uses words with restraint, and a man of understanding is even-tempered" (Proverbs 17:27, NIV).

17. CHOOSE BOLDNESS

Ready, set, go! Let boldness show.

"Do not merely listen to the word . . . do what it says" (James 1:22, NIV).

"When I called you, you answered me; you made me bold and stouthearted" (Psalm 138:3, NIV).

"A wise man has great power, and a man of knowledge increases strength" (Proverbs 24:5, NIV).

18. CHOOSE FORGIVENESS

God forgives you, so you forgive too.

"You are kind and forgiving, O Lord, abounding in love to all who call to you" (Psalm 86:5, NIV).

"Do not say, 'I will pay you back for this wrong!' Wait for the LORD, and He will deliver you" (Proverbs 20:22, NIV).

"Love your enemies and pray for those who persecute you" (Matthew 5:44, NIV).

"Bless those who persecute you; bless and do not curse" (Romans 12:14, NIV).

"And when you stand praying, if you hold anything against anyone, forgive him, so that your Father in heaven may forgive you your sins" (Mark 11:25, NIV).

19. CHOOSE DILIGENCE

Again and again, the diligent win.

"Diligent hands will rule, but laziness ends in slave labor" (Proverbs 12:24, NIV).

"Lazy hands make a man poor, but diligent hands bring wealth" (Proverbs 10:4, NIV).

"Like the coolness of snow at harvest time is a trustworthy

messenger to those who send him; he refreshes the spirit of his masters" (Proverbs 25:13, NIV).

"I have brought you glory on earth by completing the work you gave me to do" (John 17:4, NIV).

"Never tire of doing what is right" (2 Thessalonians 3:13, NIV).

"The sluggard craves and gets nothing, but the desires of the diligent are fully satisfied" (Proverbs 13:4, NIV).

20. CHOOSE CHEERFULNESS

Add some cheer to the atmosphere.

"A cheerful look brings joy to the heart" (Proverbs 15:30, NIV).

"Rejoice with those who rejoice" (Romans 12:15, NIV).

"A happy heart makes the face cheerful, but heartache crushes the spirit" (Proverbs 15:13, NIV).

"A cheerful heart is good medicine, but a crushed spirit dries up the bones" (Proverbs 17:22, NIV).

Notes

Chapter 3

1. *The Random House Dictionary of English Words,* Jess Stein, ed. (New York: Random House, 1967), p. 738.

2. Henry G. Bosch, *Our Daily Bread* (Grand Rapids, MI: Radio Bible Class, 1988), July 2.

3. *The Random House Dictionary of English Words,* p. 412.

4. James Strong, *Strong's Exhaustive Concordance of the Bible* (McLean, VA: MacDonald Publishing Company), p. 43.

5. Strong, *Strong's...Bible,* p. 43.

6. Anton Szador Lavey, *The Satanic Bible* (New York: Avon Books, 1969), pp. 30-35.

7. Joel A. Freeman, *The Doctrine of Fools* (Columbia, MD: Copy Graphics Press, 1984), pp. 7-8.

8. Martin De Haan, *Times of Discovery* (Grand Rapids, MI: Radio Bible Class, 1988), p. 1.

Chapter 5

1. "The Lighter Side," *Basically Business Newsletter* (April, 1988), p. 1.

2. This dialogue is attributed to the German philosopher Friederich Nietzsche.

Chapter 6

1. "New World," *Bottom Line* (May 30, 1988), pp. 13-14.

2. Warren Wiersbe, *Meet Your Conscience* (Wheaton, IL: Victor Books, 1983), pp. 14-23.

Chapter 7

1. *The Overlooked Requirements for Riches, Honor and Life,* Supplementary Alumni Book, Volume 13 (Oak Brook, IL: The Institute in Basic Youth Conflicts, 1987), pp. 4-11. With permission from the Institute, I borrowed freely from this volume throughout the chapter.

2. James Strong, *Strong's Exhaustive Concordance of the Bible* (McLean, VA: MacDonald Publishing Company), p. 52.

3. Noah Webster, *Webster's Third New International Dictionary* (Springfield, MA: G. & C. Merriam Company, 1966), p. 2437.

4. Strong, *Strong's...Bible,* p. 118.

5. Webster, *Webster's...Dictionary,* p. 135.

6. W. E. Vine, *An Expository Dictionary of New Testament Words* (Old Tappan, NJ: Fleming H. Revell Company, 1940), p. 52.

7. Strong, *Strong's...Bible,* p. 94.

8. *The Overlooked Requirements for Riches, Honor and Life,* p. 11.

9. Strong, *Strong's...Bible,* p. 45.

10. Strong, *Strong's...Bible,* p. 45.

11. Webster, *Webster's...Dictionary,* p. 652.

12. Strong, *Strong's...Bible,* p. 37.

13. *The Overlooked Requirements for Riches, Honor and Life,* p. 7.

14. R. C. Sproul, *The Holiness of God* (Wheaton, IL: Tyndale House Publishers, 1985), pp. 43-44.

15. Watchman Nee, *Spiritual Knowledge* (New York: Christian Fellowship Publishers, 1973), pp. 70-77.

Chapter 8
1. David Burns, *Feeling Good* (New York: Signet Books, 1980), pp. 256-257.

Chapter 9
1. Keith Green, "The Error of Balaam," *Last Days Newsletter* (Volume 7, Number 4, 1984), p. 30.

Chapter 10
1. J. Allen Petersen, *The Myth of Greener Grass* (Wheaton, IL: Tyndale House Publishers, 1983), pp. 26-27.

2. J. Vernon McGee, *The Only Psalm* (Los Angeles, CA: The Church of the Open Door, n.d.).

Chapter 13
1. W. E. Vine, *An Expository Dictionary of New Testament Words* (Old Tappan, NJ: Fleming H. Revell Company, 1940), p. 224.

Appendix A
1. *The Overlooked Requirements for Riches, Honor and Life,* Supplementary Alumni Book, Volume 13 (Oak Brook, IL: The Institute in Basic Youth Conflicts, 1987), pp. 2-4. Used by permission.

Appendix B
1. *Choices,* provided by Rainfall, Inc., and co-developed by Joyce Farrel and Associates (Grand Rapids, MI, n.d.). Used by permission.

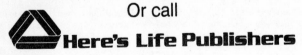